The Practice of Prayer

By

G. CAMPBELL MORGAN, D. D.

WESTMINSTER CHAPEL

Author of " The Crises of the Christ,"
" The Spirit of God," etc.

NEW YORK   CHICAGO   TORONTO

Fleming H. Revell Company

LONDON AND EDINBURGH

To

MARIANNE ADLARD

one of the hidden workers, who "endures
as seeing him who is invisible," and who
in secret labours by intercession
with those who preach the word

CONTENTS

"*And it came to pass, as He was praying in a certain place, that when He ceased, one of His disciples said unto Him, Lord, teach us to pray, even as John also taught his disciples. And He said unto them, When ye pray, say, Father, Hallowed be Thy name. Thy kingdom come. Give us day by day our daily bread. And forgive us our sins ; for we ourselves also forgive every one that is indebted to us, and bring us not into temptation.*

"*And He said unto them, Which of you shall have a friend, and shall go unto him at midnight, and say to him, Friend, lend me three loaves ; for a friend of mine is come to me from a journey, and I have nothing to set before him ; and he from within shall answer and say, Trouble me not ; the door is now shut, and my children are with me in bed ; I cannot rise and give thee ? I say unto you, Though he will not rise and give him, because he is his friend, yet because of his importunity he will arise and give him as many as he needeth. And I say unto you, Ask, and it shall be given you : seek, and ye shall find : knock, and it shall be opened unto you. For every one that asketh receiveth ; and he that seeketh findeth ; and to him that knocketh it shall be opened. And of which of you that is a father shall his son ask a loaf, and he give him a stone ? or a fish, and he for a fish give him a serpent ? Or if he shall ask an egg, will he give him a scorpion ? If ye then, being evil, know how to give good gifts unto your children, how much more shall your heavenly Father give the Holy Spirit to them that ask Him ? "*—
LUKE 11 : 1-13.

I

PRELIMINARY

NEVER did the disciples prefer a more important request than when they said "Lord, teach us to pray": and no petition was more graciously answered. The church to-day needs to bring that petition first of all, but she needs to do so remembering that she already has the answer in all spaciousness and clearness. Whatever may have been the case with the first disciples it is certainly true of us that before we "call" He "answers."

I have chosen as the general title of this book "The Practice of Prayer," because the purpose of its publication is preëminently practical. Any discussion of the doctrine of prayer which does not issue in the practice of prayer is not only not helpful, it is dangerous. At the same time that practice will be greatly helped by an apprehension of the relative Christian doctrine.

That there is need for its consideration is granted on every hand. Side by side with a great enrichment there is a wide-spread impoverishment in the Church of God. The consciousness of wealth creates the sense of poverty, and it is because we rejoice in our gain that we mourn over our lack.

As to enrichment, there can be no question that the church's appreciation of Jesus Christ is keener and more spacious to-day than it has ever been. There is to-day a wide-spread consciousness of the

11

human Christ and this has brought assurance of His interest in all departments of human life. Coincidentally with this there has arisen a conviction of His universality, and while rejoicing as never in the warmth and nearness of the Flesh, we have come to a larger apprehension of the infinitude of the Word. In practical equipment for service too the Church in men, in money, and in methods, is far in advance of any preceding age.

Yet in all these things there is a sense of lack and of poverty. While the sense of the greatness of Christ is larger, the ability to bring men into loving, saving touch with Him sometimes seems less. The men at His disposal are many, but the Church lacks energy to send them forth. Money is more freely given than ever, and yet the greater part of the possessions of the saints is still retained for their own use. The methods are multiplied, and yet one cannot help the conviction that many of our organizations are fungus growths, sapping the Church's life and contributing nothing to her fruitfulness.

We are profoundly conscious of lack. Everywhere there is a double sense, that of power and of paralysis. We have heard the sound of the going in the top of the mulberry trees, but the wind of God seems to tarry. We saw the flaming of the bush among the Welsh mountains a little while ago, but we have seen it in England. All about us are indifferent masses. We still mourn the dearth of conversions, and are painfully conscious of the languishing missionary spirit.

Where is the lack? That is a larger question than it is the purpose of this book to discuss. Nevertheless, I think it may broadly be stated that the supreme need of the Church is the realization experimentally of her relationship to God by the Holy Spirit. In the interaction of life and prayer will be found the secret of power, and the realization of fellowship with God will never be more than a theory save as prayer becomes a practice. I am particularly anxious to write nothing censorious or that fails in recognition of all the best things still to be found against us. I am profoundly conscious that there is a great deal of prayer on the highest plane. God has His intercessors everywhere. They are to be found often in unexpected places, in men and women who have learned the secret, and who by familiar intercourse with God are channels of blessing to men : but the majority of us are not praying. While I thank God for the prayers being offered I feel that it is of the utmost importance that the whole Church should know the secret of prevailing prayer, not only as a theory, but in practice.

In the presence of this need the importance of our presenting the same petition as the early disciples is apparent. That petition must be carefully understood. It was a much larger one than we too often make it. We minimize its meaning by adding to its words. They did not say, Lord, teach us how to pray, but, " Lord, teach us to pray." A great many people know how to pray, but they do not pray. The request, Teach us how to pray,

would refer simply to the theory. The petition
"teach us to pray," is of much fuller import and
includes theory and practice.

It is interesting to notice the circumstances in
which the disciples preferred this request. "And
it came to pass, as He was praying in a certain
place, that when He ceased, one of His disciples
said unto Him, Lord, teach us to pray." It is
hardly possible to read these words without seeing the connection between their request and
their observation of the Lord. Jesus Himself
was preëminently a man of prayer, and there is
no doubt that they had often seen Him at prayer,
in all probability had heard Him. Although He
never prayed with them or used of His own
prayers the same words He used of theirs, yet it
was clearly manifest to them how much prayer
meant to Him, and it is as though they had said,
" We would come into this secret of Thine." It
was a request arising from their conviction of the
value of prayer in His life.

The answer of Jesus was far more comprehensive than at first sight may appear. Immediately He gave them a pattern and a parable.
The pattern itself was not exhaustive, for it consisted of the recitation of certain sentences from
the form of prayer included in His Manifesto.
He then gave them a parable which taught by
contrast the readiness of God to hear and answer. If through importunity, is the answer,
they could be persuaded to give, how much more
would God give out of the love of His heart.

This pattern and parable, however, constitute nothing more than the local, immediate and partial answer of Jesus to their request. Later He gave them much detailed teaching in His paschal discourses, and yet not even this final teaching exhausted His great and gracious answer. He is Himself, in His revelation of the place and power of prayer in human life, the supreme answer to their request. By the whole fact of incarnation and perfect life, of atonement, resurrection and perpetual priesthood does Christ answer this preliminary prayer.

It is well for us to remember that we are in direct succession to these disciples, that their requests are our requests, and His answers to them are His answers to us. Making all allowance for a distinguishing between things which differ, between matters which pertain to the specific message of the early days of Jesus and matters connected with the commission under which we serve; it still remains true that His essential teaching was intended for us as well as for those who first heard it. When He stood surrounded by that first group of disciples He prayed, and in the course of His prayer He said, "Neither for these only do I pray, but for them also that believe on Me through their word." I always feel warmly near to the heart of Christ when I read these words, for I know that He saw me also, and included me in His priestly intercession. As there He prayed for us with them, so also in all His teaching He spoke to us as to them.

"*He that cometh to God must believe that He is, and that He is a rewarder of them that seek after Him.*" —HEBREWS 11 : 7.

"*If ye abide in Me, and My words abide in you, ask whatsoever ye will, and it shall be done unto you.*"—JOHN 15 : 7.

"*And they continued stedfastly in the Apostles' teaching and fellowship, in the breaking of bread and the prayers.*"—ACTS 2 : 42.

II

THE POSSIBILITY OF PRAYER

WHILE the purpose of the present series of studies is that of stating the positive truth of the Christian faith concerning prayer, it is necessary at least to recognize the fact that among the things of weakness characterizing our age is a far spread doubt of the possibility of prayer. It is affirmed that the advance of scientific knowledge has made it impossible to believe that the desires and petitions of individual souls or of companies in agreement can have any effect upon the affairs of a universe conditioned absolutely within law. Some there are, therefore, and those the more consistent, who abandon prayer in every form, while others urge the maintenance of the habit of prayer because of the effect it produces upon those who pray. These claim that prayer, while devoid of objective value, has yet a subjective value. It is not my purpose to attempt any philosophical discussion on this question. I believe that the majority of persons who read will concede at once the objective value of prayer, and I do not think anything said in defense of the theory will bring conviction to those in doubt. It is only by praying that the possibility is proven. He has proved the objective value of prayer who has asked and received, who has sought and found, who has knocked and known the door opened in answer. Yet there are certain of the simplest things which may be said in this connection.

Let it once be granted that prayer has a subjective value and it will be difficult to escape conviction of its objective value. If it be true that petition has produced an effect upon character which is uplifting and ennobling, then that effect is due to belief in the existence of One who hears and is able to grant requests. If there be no such possibility, then belief in that which is untrue issues in character which is true and beautiful. This is unthinkable. All the subjective value of prayer has grown out of conviction of an objective value. If a man asks for something, it is because he believes he can obtain it by asking. Once persuade a man that it is impossible for him to receive an answer to his petition and he will not persist in asking. Thus will the subjective value of prayer be inevitably destroyed when the objective value is denied. No man will continue to ask if he be once convinced that his asking has no greater value than that it produces an effect upon himself. Everything which man has observed of the subjective value of prayer, of the influence it has produced upon character and tone, has been due to profound conviction of its objective value. Sincere and honest men who once deny the objective value cease praying, witness such men as Darwin, Tyndal, Spencer and Huxley. Their philosophy led them to the conclusion that prayer was never answered and therefore they properly and honestly—though as we think—mistakenly and disastrously ceased to pray.

I am not for a single moment denying the subjective value of prayer. No human being has ever lived the life of familiarity with the secret place without bearing the light and glory of it on the face. Those who know what it is to talk often with God gain a tone in their talking with men which cannot be mistaken. Herein the subjective value of prayer, but it came out of profound conviction that when they spoke they were heard, when they asked they were answered. I believe therefore that the demonstration of the subjective value of prayer is presumptive evidence of its objective value.

Our belief, however, in the prevailing power of prayer has firmer foundations. It is based first of all upon our doctrine of God. We do not believe that He is the slave of His own laws. At the same time we do not believe in a God who is lawless, but law-abiding. His knowledge of all law is, however, such as to enable Him in the overruling of one law by another so to perform what to our limited vision appears to be miraculous. Our doctrine of God makes us believe that it is possible for Him to do in answer to prayer that which appears to be contrary to law, but which is in reality wrought by the operation of a law of which we know nothing in relation to another law of which we know something. It is reasonable that those who deny the possibility of prayer always deny the existence of the miraculous. What is a miracle? The word simply means something which surprises, something for which we cannot account. Now, the only reason why men deny the possibility of prayer is that they deny the possibility of things which they cannot understand. That is the meaning of the denial of everything which we call supernatural. Our doctrine of God affirms that from the standpoint of His existence, of His government, of His love, there is nothing supernatural. The things which appear to be supernatural to me, are natural to Him. Every miracle of the New Testament and of the Old Testament was a simple happening which surprised men who did not know all the facts and forces of the universe. Those things surprising to finite men were actions perfectly natural to God. It is surely time that we recognize this. A great many things of which our fathers would have spoken as being quite as miraculous as anything recorded in the Bible, are commonplaces of every-day life to us. We are not surprised at the wonders wrought by electricity because we have discovered laws of which our fathers knew nothing. Yet the increase of our knowledge makes us the more ready to declare that even to-day we are but children of the dawn. The Christian affirmation is that God dwells in the light and there is no darkness with Him. That which appears to contradict nature is in harmony with the whole economy of God, and the work of God within the realm of laws higher than those which man has yet discovered. It may be objected that law cannot overrule law; but experience proves the contrary. I hold a book in my hand. The law of gravitation demands its fall but it remains in my hand because of the operation of an overruling law. In all the simplest things of life this inter-action of law is at work. Now, the Christian doctrine of God declares that He sitteth at the centre of the universe. He rules eternity with His presence. All laws are but His thoughts, and He is able to call into operation force against force, law against law. We therefore believe it is possible for His children to go to Him and ask of Him and receive from Him things they cannot obtain in any other way. Things absolutely impossible to men within the realm of the laws they know may become possible to them, if they can gain His ear and touch His Heart and find the answer of His overruling power. Once deny that God can answer prayer, and He is degraded into a being less than His universe, a prisoner in the heart of His own creation.

Again, our belief in the possibility of prayer is based upon the declarations of Jesus, and behind His declarations there is Himself. If when I ask I never have; when I seek I cannot find; when I knock no door is opened to me, then either Christ was deceived or a deceiver. His teaching was most explicit. In this connection one quotation, perhaps the most remarkable of all, will

suffice. "If ye abide in Me, and My words abide
in you, ask whatsoever ye will, and it shall be
done unto you." A careful examination of that
passage makes it even more wonderful than appears at first sight. The word "ask" may with
perfect accuracy be rendered "demand as your
due." No violence will be done to the Lord's
words if instead of " whatsoever ye will " we read
" whatsoever ye are inclined to." Yet again, the
word translated "done," may be changed into
"generated," and we have here as it seems to me,
the most stupendous statement regarding prayer
ever uttered. It makes prayer limitless within
limits. "If ye abide in Me, and My words abide
in you," are the limits. Let these be observed,
then prayer becomes the method of coöperation
with Deity. The life of true relation to Himself is
one in which desire harmonizes with the purposes
of God, and which therefore demands an answer
which is provided even though the creative force
of Deity should be employed. If there is no
answer to prayer, then these are the words of
One who was deceived, or was a deceiver—impossible alternatives despite a thousand new-born
philosophies. Neither was He deceived, nor a
deceiver. What He said is true though the
heavens fall. Heaven and earth may pass away,
but His word cannot. To deny the possibility of
prayer is to deny the teaching of Jesus. To deny
that teaching is to destroy Him.

Yet once again, we base our belief in the possibility of prayer upon the history and experi-

ence of men. When science makes experience the
universal test of reality how can men rationally
exclude the experience of the saints of all ages in
this matter? They tell us they have asked and
had; sought and found; knocked and the door
has been opened. In answer to this it is affirmed
that they were all perfectly sincere in believing
so, but they were mistaken. Such a statement
is a test of patience to which I am not equal. To
be told that not one or two; but hundreds, thousands, tens of thousands of human beings, not of
one age or temperament or geographical position; but in every age, of all temperaments and
from every clime, though weeks and months and
years and decades and centuries and millenniums,
have all been deceived, is to be asked to believe
something far more incredible than anything
which Christianity affirms as true. If the testimony of seers, prophets, psalmists, saints, confess-
ors and martyrs is all to go for nothing; yet
may God help me to share their delusion, for it
has been a glorious delusion and the dynamic by
which all the best work of the centuries has been
done. We affirm therefore, our belief in the objective value of prayer, first because of our doctrine of God; secondly because of the declarations of Jesus Christ, and finally because of the
history and the experience of the saints.

Yet, let me go one step further. God has been
reached always through His Son, Jesus Christ.
Not that men have always understood this, not
that we perfectly understand it to-day, but the

fact remains that fallen man has always found his way to God in prayer through the mystery of the mediation of Christ. Now, that is the theme we are proposing to follow. The Christian revelation is that of the constant method by which man has been able to pray ; by which man has asked and received, has sought and found ; has knocked and found the door opened. So that the final proof of the objective value of prayer lies in all that Christian economy which we claim creates its possibility, and which is to be considered.

"*No man hath seen God at any time; but the only begotten Son, which is in the bosom of the Father, He hath declared Him.*"—JOHN 1 : 18.

"*He that cometh from above is above all; he that is of the earth is of the earth, and of the earth he speaketh : He that cometh from heaven is above all What He hath seen and heard, of that He beareth witness; and no man receiveth His witness. He that hath received His witness hath set His seal to this, that God is true.*"—JOHN 3 · 31-33.

"*I am the good Shepherd : the good Shepherd layeth down His life for the sheep. . . . Therefore doth the Father love Me, because I lay down My life, that I may take it again. No one taketh it away from Me, but I lay it down of Myself. I have power to lay it down, and I have power to take it again This commandment received I from My Father.*"—JOHN 10 · 11, 17, 18.

"*Verily, verily, I say unto you, He that believeth on Me, the works that I do shall he do also ; and greater works than these shall he do : because I go unto the Father. And whatsoever ye shall ask in My name, that will I do, that the Father may be glorified in the Son. If ye shall ask Me anything in My name, that will I do.*"—JOHN 14 · 12-14.

"*And I will pray the Father, and He shall give you another Comforter, that He may be with you forever, even the Spirit of truth · whom the world cannot receive; for it beholdeth Him not, neither knoweth Him · ye know Him; for He abideth with you, and shall be in you. . . . But the Comforter, even the Holy Spirit, whom the Father will send in My name, He shall teach you all things, and bring to your remembrance all that I said unto you.*"—JOHN 14 : 16, 17, 26.

"*But when the Comforter is come, whom I will send unto you from the Father, even the Spirit of truth, which proceedeth from the Father, He shall bear witness of Me.*"—JOHN 15. 26.

III

THE PLATFORM OF PRAYER

HAVING considered the subject of the possibility of prayer generally, we now proceed to think of it particularly, and as within the Christian fact. In the three groups of Scriptures with which this study is prefaced we have indicated the threefold fact which creates the possibility of prayer according to Christian teaching and experience. The selection of verses is not intended to be exhaustive. It would be quite possible to take other single verses containing the same truth in some other setting. It is also self-evident that in this study there is no intention of dealing exhaustively with the verses selected. I propose only to deduce from them their suggestiveness on this particular subject of prayer.

In the first place let me state the general value of each group. In the first our Lord is presented to us as the One who has revealed the Father. In the second He is presented as the One who brings us, through His mediatorial work, into the presence of the Father that there we may appear complete in the Son, and therefore unafraid. In the third He is presented to us as the One through whose perfect and accomplished work the Spirit is given to us to abide with us, to be in us.

29

This threefold fact creates the Christian platform of prayer. Its first phase is that Christ has made such a revelation of the Father as creates in our hearts a desire for prayer. The second is that He has done such work for us as admits us to the presence of God in order that we may have the right to pray. While the third is that upon the accomplishment of His work and as its crowning glory He poured forth His Spirit who by indwelling is the inspiration of our prayer as we stand in Christ in the presence of that God whom Jesus has perfectly revealed.

The relation of this threefold fact to our previous study should be noted. Therein we declared that we believe prayer to be possible because of our doctrine of God. From whence did we obtain this doctrine? From Christ's revelation of the Father. We declared in the second place, that we believe prayer to be possible because of the teaching of Christ. What was the final teaching of Christ in answer to that request of His disciples? It was not the teaching of His words, but that of His work. The meditation of Jesus is His ultimate teaching which brings conviction to our hearts of the possibility of prayer. Finally, we declared that we believe in the possibility of prayer because of the experience of the saints. How has that experience been created? It has ever been the result of the indwelling and inspiration of the Holy Spirit.

Let us now approach the subject from another standpoint, by asking whether prayer is possible

apart from these truths. I unhesitatingly reply
that it is not. If they are denied prayer will
cease sooner or later. There may be prayer in
some senses apart from a consciousness of these
things. There is an instinct for prayer in human
nature which expresses itself among all peoples;
but prayer, as we understand it, as our fathers
have experienced it, and as the New Testament
teaches, is absolutely impossible save on that
platform. Let us begin with the first fact. Suppose it were possible to blot out the revelation
of God which the Word- has received through
Jesus Christ. The supposition is of course an
absurdity. The revelation can never be entirely
lost. It has become ingrained in the common
consciousness of the age. Those who deny the
deity of Jesus and tell us they believe in the
Fatherhood of God speaking with exquisite
beauty of that fatherhood, are speaking of that
which Christ revealed. For the sake of argument,
however, let us suppose it possible that the world
should lose that consciousness of God which
Christ has created, what then would be the result?
The measure of intellectual progress apart from
revelation would be the measure in which men
would cease to pray. It may be objected that
this is to declare that prayer is not an intellectual
exercise, but that is not so. When I refer to the
measure of man's intellectual progress apart from
revelation I am proposing to omit the quantity
without which the intellect is at once darkened
and imprisoned. No man is a full grown intel-

lectual who is not ready to receive revelation. To turn the back upon revelation is necessarily to cease to pray. Why did Huxley, Tyndal, Darwin and Spencer cease to pray? The answer inevitably is, because they ceased to believe in revealed religion; they denied that God had revealed Himself to men directly and specifically. Some declared that He was unknowable, that it was not possible for Him to reveal Himself to men or for men to receive any revelation from Him. Denying revealed religion, they turned to nature and prosecuted their inquiry with absolute honesty and splendid devotion. Some of their number, as we well know, who in their early days possessed a love of poetry and music, lost it entirely in their devotion to cold scientific investigation. What was their ultimate position? They could not pray. And this, because nature never reveals that fact concerning God which creates desire for prayer. Nature does reveal God, but not in all the facts of His Being. What can a man find in nature if he shuts the book of revelation, and declines to believe that God has spoken in His Word or through His Son? The Apostle, writing to the Romans, declared that God had evidently revealed Himself in nature in two particulars, namely in His power and divinity. The men to whom reference has been made declared that they found at the back of all natural phenomena an eternal energy. One of them spoke of this as "a double-faced somewhat, a combination of intelligence and force." I

accept the testimony of the Apostle and of the
modern scientist, that you find God in nature as
force and as intelligence, but to neither of these,
nor to the two in coöperation, is it possible to
pray. I cannot pray to force. All I can do in
its presence is to discover its law and obey it in
order that I may constrain it to serve me rather
than to blast me. It is a perpetual law of force
that it will do the one or the other according to
the relation which we bear to it. Take dynamite
as expressive of force. To disobey its law is to
be scattered by it into fragments. By obedience
to its law is the rock blasted and the highway
created. When men would use dynamite they
do not pray to it. They discover its law. If
God be only an eternal energy, then I cannot
pray, but even then I will attempt to discover the
law of His operation and obey it. During the
last fifty years man's conception of the divine
intelligence has been greatly enlarged. As man
has prosecuted his inquiry and come to understand more perfectly the marvel of the universe
in the midst of which he lives, he has come to a
larger comprehension of the marvel of the all-
governing intelligence. For instance, there was a
time when man turned his telescope to the
heavens and counted the stars. A little later on
with a more powerful instrument he declared that
the number was far in excess of that first
affirmed; until at last Rosse turned his great re-
fractor to the heavens and declared that the stars
cannot be counted. That is the scientific posi-

tion to-day. The Bible affirmed it long ago. Jeremiah sang that the stars were without number, but men declared it was the license of poetry. As a matter of fact it was cold, hard, scientific fact. To return, however, this scientific investigation has enlarged man's conception of the intelligence behind nature, and in that proportion it has been less easy for man to pray. That may sound a strange thing to say, and yet I think it must be conceded as true. When I find illimitable intelligence ordering seasons and marshalling stars I cannot believe that by any asking of mine I can hope to affect or persuade such a mind. I cannot pray to intelligence.

But now I read "No man hath seen God at any time; the only begotten Son, which is in the bosom of the Father, He hath declared Him." Here is a new quantity, a new fact, "the bosom of the Father." Put this into other words and read, "the heart of God." Jesus has revealed the fact that God is more than force and intelligence working in coöperation. He is a personal Being, and at the back of the force presiding over it, behind the intelligence inspiring it, is love. If that be true there is at once born within me a desire to pray. If it be true that behind all the rest there is a heart, then I will pray in spite of force, and notwithstanding intelligence. If God is but another name for intelligence, that intelligence is demonstrated to be so stupendous that it is unthinkable and foolish for me to attempt to pray to such a mind as that.

Prayer is impossible. I am bruised and broken
upon life's highway but there is no help for me
in the inscrutable might and mind of which I am
conscious. But out of the infinite spaces there
comes to me a great love song. Out of the bosom
of the Father comes a message of tenderness and
compassion. Immediately, bruised and broken
as I am, I want to pray. I desire to speak out
of my sense of sin and sorrow to the heart behind force and intelligence concerning my need.
Agony can sob itself out upon a heart. Impo-
tence can trust love. A sinner can turn his face
back towards a Father. Neither force nor intelligence, nor both working in coöperation constitute God. If that is all a man knows of God
he will cease to speak of it as God, and presently
will write the word with a small g, or he will
simply use the word in accommodation to the age
in which he lives, not because of its personal significance. Christ has revealed to men the fact
that the personality behind the universe is force,
intelligence and heart, a complete personality, not
only volitional and intellectual but emotional
withal. While I cannot comprehend Him nor
encompass Him within my finite thinking, I still
know that I have found in that infinite conception something which perfectly corresponds to
my finite life. There is something in me of force
and intelligence, but the greatest of me is my
heart. When my finite heart finds the infinite
heart of God I am able to trust my finite
strength to His infinite strength, and my finite

mind to His infinite intelligence. This then is the first fact in the platform of prayer, that the God of the universe has a bosom, a heart, and that the Son has spoken to men out of it. By the way of Jesus Christ there has come to man this new revelation concerning God, the revelation of His heart, of His essential essence, of His love. Out of that revelation is born the passion for prayer in the soul of man.

Yet that fact alone does not make prayer possible, neither does it reveal to us the platform upon which we stand to pray. Though I appear to contradict what I have already said it must be affirmed that in the moment when I stand face to face with God as the God of love, even though the desire to pray is born within me I am conscious that I dare not pray. When Jesus Christ brings me into His presence and I find His love, there is immediately in my nature a going out after Him; but simultaneously with the birth of desire comes a new consciousness which seals my lips. It is when I stand in the presence of God as love that I realize for the first time the real meaning of sin, and I am silent. This assertion may not carry conviction at first, yet think of it! The men who have missed the vision of God's love have invariably lost their sense of their own sin. Those who have lost the God of revelation never speak of sin as do those who live in the light of revelation. Sin to the former is an infirmity, a weakness, a process of development. It has recently been affirmed that this is an age

in which men of highly developed intelligence
do not care to think of or speak of sin, but it is
surely no proof of high development that men
desire to close their eyes to facts.   I repeat, that
to lose the vision of God is to lose the sense of
sin.   If I simply think of an eternal energy
working in response to supreme intelligence, I
become conscious of my own weakness and my
own foolishness, but never of my sin.   It is when
I stand in the presence of the heart of God that
I really begin to know what sin is.   To illustrate
briefly from personal experience.   I was born in
a Christian home, nurtured by Christian parents,
and by that fact graciously and tenderly spared
from many of the vulgarities of godlessness.
Consequently Mount Sinai with its thunder
never made me tremble, never brought deep conviction of sin to my heart.   I have always sym-
pathized with the young ruler who confronted
by the six final words of the decalogue, could
yet look into the face of incarnate purity and
say, "All these things have I observed from my
youth."   But when I came to stand consciously,
not at the foot of the mount which might not
be touched, but on the green hill outside the city
wall, and saw in the mystery of that passion and
pain the revelation of the heart of God, the self-
sacrificing, self-denying heart of God, I knew
what a sinner I was.   When I came into the
presence of God as love I found in love a light
which bowed me to the dust in shame, and
though my sad heart yearned to pray, I dared

not take His name upon my lips, for He is love
ineffable who has—let me say it reverently—denied Himself in order to help men. In the light
of that love I discovered that sin does not consist
in incidental acts of passing days, but in the essential attitude of selfishness. It is when Jesus
brings me into the presence of the heart of God
that I put my hand upon my lips and cry, Unclean, unclean. I want to pray. I dare not
pray. I have forfeited all right to ask for anything from such love. I need yet more than the
revelation of the Father before I can pray.
Thank God there is more.

I pass to the second group of Scriptures and in
them I find the provision I seek. "I am the
good Shepherd: the good Shepherd layeth down
His life for the sheep." Death and resurrection
are in that sentence. He layeth down His life, that
is the mystery of His dying. He layeth down His
life for the sheep, that is, in such a way that it
becomes communicate to them. "No one taketh it
away from Me, but I lay it down of Myself. I have
power to lay it down, and I have power to take
it again. This commandment received I from
My Father." Thus in the radiant splendour of
these words of Jesus I see One who comes out
from God, lays down His life, and in the mystery
of that act clears me from sin, who takes His life
again in resurrection and in the might of that act
places at my disposal a new life which makes it
possible for me to stand unafraid in the presence
of God. All this is exactly what I need. I cannot pray unless my sin is forgiven and my dead

spiritual nature is brought to life. Hear me in
solemn reverence as I speak out of my heart's
deepest consciousness. I need something done
for me whereby the pollution of sin can be blotted
out, if not for God's sake for my own. If you
could persuade me that God could forgive me
without all that the Cross means, you could not
persuade me that I could forgive myself. I must
have something that cleanses from the pollution
which spoils and harms and clings to my life.
Sentimental passion and pity cannot purge the
stain from my own conscience. In the very deepest of me there is a cry which answers the very
word of revelation, "Without the shedding of
blood there is no remission." Ere I can enter the
presence chamber of the revealed Father and
pray, I need some mystery of cleansing and healing, some new dynamic which should touch and
quicken into life the withered powers within me.
I am amazed at the love of God, but I dare not
pray until the revealing Son stands before me as
Mediator also. "Who is this that cometh from
Edom, with dyed garments from Bozrah? this
that is glorious in His apparel, marching in the
greatness of His strength?" It is One with
wounded hands, the mystery of pain written upon
His face, with all the evidences of the passion of
sacrificial dying enwrapping Him as with a pur-
ple robe. Who is He? He is the Son, the good
Shepherd. The One who came after lost ones.
The One who found them bruised and broken;
mangled and torn by wolves. The One who laid
down His life to rescue them, and yet in such

power as to be able to take it again and communicate it to them so that it became their life. The One who by such dying and living has given to men of His life the vision, the virtue, the victory. It is God Himself acting out in the limitation of time and sense and flesh that infinite mystery of love saving through sacrifice. Thus it is through the rent veil of His flesh that I enter the place of prayer. It is through the mystery of His accomplished work that I dare to draw near. I who had felt the moving of God's heart as Jesus spake and taught and yet was made afraid thereby because of sin, am now brought near by the mystery of mediation and in the presence of God I dare to pray, standing unafraid in the light of God's love in the merit and might of the death and resurrection of His Son.

And yet once again, I cannot pray. The love of God revealed has made me desire to pray. The work of Jesus as Mediator has brought me into the place of prayer, but I was never more afraid to pray than now. That is the meaning of the Apostolic declaration, " We know not how to pray as we ought." For who are these of whom he thus speaks? They are the people whose experience is described in the chapter which commences with " no condemnation," and ends with " no separation." There is surely no time in which a man feels less able to pray than when having seen the vision of God through Jesus, and having been made nigh by Jesus to God, he stands in the place where he is free to pray. The nearer we live to the heart of Jesus, and the closer we abide in the consciousness of God's love the less shall we feel able to pray.   We sometimes sing

> The weakest, feeblest need the most
> The praying in the Holy Ghost.

That is a great truth, and yet I think it may be written in another way,

> The strongest, mightiest need the most
> The praying in the Holy Ghost.

That is to say those who have answered the revelation of love by absolute abandonment to the mediating Son; those who have entered most perfectly into the experience of the Divine provision, need most sorely a true inspiration, and are the most acutely conscious of their need.   To stand in the presence of such love by such grace is to shrink back lest by some impurity of motive or faultiness of desire prayer should become unworthy.

Thus we are brought to the third fact in the provision for prayer, that was dealt with in the final discourses of Jesus when He promised the Comforter.   The indwelling Spirit interprets to us the meaning of the life we live and gives us to see the will of God in Jesus, and the way in which we must act in order to realize that will. The indwelling Spirit who knows the will of God creates our new aspirations and desires, and out of these comes our prayer.   Thus standing in the light of the revealed Father through the mediation of His Son and answering the inspiration of the indwelling Spirit we pray.

In conclusion let these thoughts be summarized.

By the coming of Jesus God has been so revealed
as to create the desire for prayer. By the work
of Jesus mediation has been made which brings
man into the place of prayer. By the indwelling
of Jesus by the Spirit desires are created and
choices are made which express themselves in
prayer. Thus through the mercy of the Father,
the merit of the mediating Son, and the might of
the inspiring Spirit, prayer is possible. That conception of the platform of prayer must have an
effect upon our praying. If we lack that vision we
shall pray ignorantly and foolishly. We shall
ask and have not because we ask amiss. If once
that platform of prayer be recognized and we understand to whom, and through whom and by
whom we pray, our praying will become prevailing. The whole truth may be constantly remembered by the Apostolic benediction, "The grace
of the Lord Jesus Christ, and the love of God,
and the communion of the Holy Spirit." The
only difference is that in this benediction we commence with the grace of the Lord Jesus Christ
and then pass to that infinite fountain, the love
of God, and finally refer to that abiding fellowship, the communion of the Holy Spirit. "The
grace of the Lord Jesus Christ," "though He was
rich, yet for your sakes He became poor, that ye
through His poverty might become rich." That
is the story of mediation. "The love of God,"
that is the whole word of Christ's revelation.
"The communion of the Holy Spirit," that is the
fact of the Spirit's indwelling and inspiration.

" Fear not, little flock; for it is your Father's good pleasure to give you the Kingdom."—LUKE 12:32.

" But of Him are ye in Christ Jesus, who was made unto us wisdom from God, and righteousness and sanctification, and redemption."—1 CORINTHIANS 1.30.

" For we know that the whole creation groaneth and travaileth in pain together until now. And not only so, but ourselves also, which have the first-fruits of the Spirit, even we ourselves groan within ourselves, waiting for our adoption, to wit, the redemption of our body. For by hope we were saved; but hope that is seen is not hope: for who hopeth for that which he seeth? But if we hope for that which we see not, then do we with patience wait for it. And in like manner the Spirit also helpeth our infirmity: for we know not how to pray as we ought; but the Spirit Himself maketh intercession for us with groanings which cannot be uttered; and He that searcheth the hearts knoweth what is in the mind of the Spirit, because He maketh intercession for the saints according to the will of God. And we know that to them that love God all things work together for good, even to them that are called according to His purpose."—ROMANS 8:22-28.

IV

THE PREPARATION FOR PRAYER

LET me at once clear the ground by making plain what I do not mean by preparation for prayer. In this title there is no reference to any preparation which is occasional and special. For such preparation there will be no necessity in proportion as the larger preparation of the life is assured. It is a great question whether the attitude of mind which demands some recall and readjustment in order to public or private prayer is at any time one which is honouring to our Lord and Master. I am perfectly well aware that this is a somewhat startling statement, and I appeal for a careful consideration of the subject now to be dealt with that the truth concerned, may be ascertained. In the meantime I do most confidently affirm that it ought to be a perfectly natural and easy thing to turn from work or play to prayer at any time or in any place, and moreover, it seems to me increasingly, as days pass on that any work or play which makes that spontaneous prayer impossible should be abandoned at all costs and once for all. As to private prayer, believing as I do in its required constancy I cannot also believe in the necessity for any process of preparation. As to public prayer, an illustration will express in the simplest way my entire feeling on the subject. Some few years ago in a certain city in England, which shall be nameless, in preparation for special services I met the ministers and workers in conference. In the course of an address to them I said that I should be very glad if my brethren in the ministry would be on the platform with me and be ready to lead in prayer as they were asked. At the close of the meeting one minister came to me and said, "I should be so glad if you think of asking me to pray if you will let me know the day before so that I may be prepared." I replied, "If I want you to pray I will let you know the day before." I never asked him to pray. Some may object to this, believing that a man ought to have time to prepare to pray on such an occasion. I can only say for myself that the kind of preparation which has been very largely followed in any such case has in my judgment wrought wide-spread harm. At many of our great ecclesiastical gatherings, prayers are heard which are perfect literary productions, but which lack the passion and power which prevail. Consequently I am not dealing with the subject of how to prepare for prayer upon some special occasion. If we learn the deep secrets of prayer we shall be able to pray anywhen and anywhere. We shall fulfill the injunctions of the New Testament which startle us—Christ's injunction, "Men ought always to pray," and the Apostolic injunction, "Pray without ceasing." Too often our method of dealing with such texts is a revelation of our unpreparedness for prayer. We say Christ did not really mean that men ought always to pray. He meant that they ought to pray as often as they can. He meant nothing of the kind. When He said, "Men ought always to pray," He meant it. When the Holy Spirit speaking through the Apostle said "Pray without ceasing," He meant it. If we can but learn the true secret of preparation we shall find that our whole life becomes prayer, that it will be impossible for us to write a letter without a lifting of the heart to God for guidance. I am inclined to think that the more we know of real prayer the less time we may spend in the external and apparent exercise thereof.

I am speaking then of the preparation which touches life, and so makes us ready for prayer at all times. Having thus attempted to clear the ground let me proceed. I propose first to put the whole statement into one brief sentence, and then examine that sentence in detail. The whole case then may thus be stated.

Preparation for prayer is secured by response in the life to the great facts which make prayer possible.

That I maintain is the inclusive philosophy of preparation for prayer. Now let us examine that statement. First of all it must be remembered that all truth is a light which reveals a pathway in which man must walk. Truth always sets up a claim, makes a demand. It is never merely a commodity which can be stored and labelled and

shelved.   A man cannot hold truth.   Truth must
hold the man.   Immediately truth presents itself
to a life it makes a demand upon that life.   While
that is so in regard to all truth it is preeminently
the case in regard to spiritual truth.   Every truth
of the Christian faith taken hold of by the mind
makes a call upon the will.   In proportion as
that claim is answered the life is sanctified.   I
hold the truth which holds me.   Take that principle and apply it to this subject of prayer.   We
have seen that the platform of prayer consists of
the threefold fact of the revelation of the Father,
the mediation of the Son, the inspiration of the
Spirit.   I am prepared for prayer in proportion
as I obey the claims set up upon my life by the
revelation of the Father; in proportion as I yield
myself to the claims made upon my life by the
mediation of the Son; in proportion as .my life
answers the claims set up within me by the
Spirit's indwelling and inspiration.   I see the
truth about God revealed in Jesus and that truth
makes claims upon me.   If I answer them I am
by such answer prepared for prayer.   I am
brought into the place where I see the truth concerning Christ's great mediatorial work.   If I
answer the claim that truth makes upon me I am
prepared for prayer.   I see the truth concerning
the Spirit's method of making intercession.   If I
answer that indwelling illumination, yield myself
to it, refuse to quench, or resist or grieve the
Spirit, and allow my life to be borne along by
the great currents of the river of God, I shall

be prepared to pray, bound to pray, and shall always pray. In other words, preparation for prayer is the life lived in harmony with the truth we profess to believe. It is not spasmodic, occasional; but lies rather in the preparation of the life itself and in proportion as we are living as we ought to live, we not only want to pray, we are able to pray : we not only want to pray and are able to pray, but we do pray, and that so as to prevail.

Let us consider this more particularly by application of the principle in the case of the previous study, our platform of prayer. We saw it to be of threefold significance, including the revelation of the Father, the mediation of the Son, the inspiration of the Spirit. If it be true that we are prepared for prayer as we respond to the great truths suggested by those words, we now have to ask ourselves, "What is the revelation of the Father; what the mediation of the Son; what the inspiration of the Spirit ?" We need to examine these things in order to find out how far we are responsive to them, how far we are obedient, so that thus we may find out how far we are really prepared for prayer. Such questions, of course, finally involve the study of the whole of Christian doctrine : but for our present practical purpose a less comprehensive inquiry will suffice. I have therefore selected the passages with which this study is prefaced, not to consider the specific teaching of each passage, but because they contain light which will help us.

Take the first of them, " Fear not, little flock ;
for it is your Father's good pleasure to give you
the Kingdom." These are the actual words of
Jesus. I am not dealing with the message of en-
couragement they contain, great and gracious as
it is and having some bearing on our subject of
prayer, as it has. I desire rather to look at the
verse from a purely literary standpoint, and in so
doing we find that Jesus recognizes all the
essential truth concerning God which He came to
reveal to man. Sometimes in ordinary conversa-
tion a very general statement will reveal the
speaker's whole philosophy on a certain subject.
When Jesus uttered these words He was not in-
tending to make a revelation of the Father, but
His conception of God flashes forth in great
clearness and beauty. If such a statement ap-
peared in a press issue from the pen of a modern
author, a merely literary critic might be tempted
to find a great deal of fault with it. I can imagine him saying, " Our author has fallen into a
strange mixture of metaphors. He begins, 'Fear
not, little flock,' and the figure in his mind is
evidently that of the shepherd and his sheep ;
but forgetting this, he continues, 'it is your
Father's good pleasure,' showing that he has
already mixed the figure of the shepherd and the
sheep with that of the father and the family ; and
again immediately he seems to have forgotten the
previous figures as he continues 'to give you the
Kingdom.'" We know perfectly that the metaphors of Jesus never clash. In this saying there

is a perfect unfolding of all the truth concerning
God which Jesus came to teach man. He is revealed as the Shepherd, Father, King. The
picture suggested is purely Eastern, and there can
be no doubt that in many respects, Eastern conditions explain fundamental positions far more
clearly than many of our Western methods do.
In the Arab tribe the Sheik is at once shepherd
of the flock, father of the family and king of the
nation. In those figures as Jesus used them He
takes us back to the original ideal of government.
Through the picture of the ancient economy He
reveals the eternal verities of which the material
things are but the shadow upon time's surface.
We must remember that these words were spoken
to His own. When He addresses those outside
He calls them first to submission to the Kingship
of God. No man ever found God as Father until
He recognized Him as King. In speaking to His
own the Master begins with the thought of the
Shepherd, then passes to that of the Father, and
finally to that of the King. At the heart of the
revelation is the thought of the Fatherhood. We
shall see that more clearly when we come to deal
with the pattern prayer, the whole of which is
addressed to the Father, the first half asking for
the setting up of the Kingdom, and the last for
the care and provision of the Shepherd. None of
these things were new. There is nothing in the
Gospels which had not been said in the Scriptures
of the old economy. Yet everything He said was
new. Men had said, " The Lord is my Shep-

herd" for ages, but when He said "I am the good Shepherd" men understood as they had never done before. In the midst of trouble, men had constantly sung "Like as a father pitieth his children, so the Lord pitieth them that fear Him," but when Jesus said " Your Father knoweth," He revealed the meaning of Fatherhood far more perfectly than the song which spoke of His pity merely. Men had recognized Jehovah as King, but Jesus came to reveal the meaning of His Kingship. Nothing was new. Everything was new. The old things blossomed into new beauty such as humanity had never dreamed of.

It is only in proportion as we answer the claims of this revelation that we are prepared for prayer. As we are loyal to the King, like unto the Father, content with the provision of the Shepherd, we are ready to pray. All this is surely self-evident. How can we pray "Thy Kingdom come," if we are rebelling against the King? How is it that our prayer so often fails to prevail? Because we persist in praying, quite honestly, " Thy Kingdom come " and yet in our own heart we are not submissive to the King. Something in the life is permitted which is contrary to His will; something in the business, the friendships, the amusements. It is a solemn, yet awful truth that we blaspheme when we pray for the Kingdom to come and will not permit it to obtain in our own life. It is an infinitely worse thing that I should pray for God's Kingdom to come in the world while I refuse to allow it to be set up in my heart, than it is to take His name in vain because I was born in a slum and had never learned to revere it.   If prayer is not prevailing in our experience it is not because some scientific teacher has denied its possibility, but rather because we are not responding to the revelation. Of the significance of the Shepherd I would speak in all tenderness.   It is when I am resting in my Shepherd's provision that I am able to pray.   If I am rebellious against my lot and persist in looking upon my work as drudgery, I cannot pray. It is the heart at leisure from itself because perfectly content with the Shepherd's provision, that is able to pray.   If I can truly say that where'er my Shepherd leads I am content because He leads ; if through the desert, I am glad, for that is best if 'tis His Will; or if He leads by waters still, I sing, not because the waters are still and the pastures green, but because He leads; then I am able to pray.   I pray God to teach me that.

Jesus revealed God as Father.   This fact is central and final.   How do we respond to it ?   A child responds to fatherhood when it reproduces the father's likeness.   That is something infinitely beyond loyalty to Kingship, or content with pasture.   The child inherits his father's nature.   If I am a child of God I inherit my Father's nature. The proportion in which I yield myself thereto until it manifests itself through me is the measure of my power to pray.   One illustration must suffice.   How can we hope to pray so as to pre-

vail while we call ourselves children of God, and
yet nurse in our hearts bitterness and malice
which are unlike God ?   It is only when God's
nature of love rules and reigns and inspires all
our life, that we shall want to pray, and that our
praying will prevail.   To use the terminology of
the praying man, is not to pray.   To have the
revelation and to answer it in loyalty to the
King, in contentment with the provision of the
Shepherd, in the reproduction of the Father's
likeness, that is to pray.

Take a step further and consider the response
of the soul to the fact of Christ's mediation.   In
his letter to the Corinthian Christians Paul had
been contrasting the wisdom of men's words with
the wisdom of the Word of the Cross.   Assuring
them that our Gospel, while a message of foolishness to the Greeks is not devoid of wisdom, in a
comprehensive statement he declares what that
wisdom is, " Of Him are ye in Christ Jesus, who
was made unto us wisdom from God, and righteousness, and sanctification and redemption."
Whether wisdom, righteousness, sanctification
and redemption are separate and differing as-
pects of our Lord's work in the believer, or
whether righteousness, sanctification and redemption are but the apostle's analysis of wisdom, the
one all-inclusive word, appears to me immaterial,
though personally I hold the latter interpretation.   Christ is wisdom, and this wisdom of God
is manifest in righteousness, sanctification and
redemption.   These three words cover the whole

fact of Christ's mediatorial work. They reveal the tenses of the Christian life. These tenses are indicated by three great words, righteousness, sanctification, redemption. The past tense of salvation is that experience to which I look back. When I believed Christ was imputed to me as righteousness. That was the salvation of my spirit. The present tense of salvation is that process through which I am now passing. Christ is being imparted to me as sanctification. That is the salvation of my mind. The future tense of salvation is the life which is nearer than when I believed. Christ will be implanted in me as redemption. That is the salvation of my body. The word translated redemption is always used with regard to the coming glory. The same word occurs in the letter to the Romans, " Even we ourselves groan within ourselves, waiting for our adoption, to wit, the redemption of our body." Of course, it will be understood that I do not mean that the English word redemption is always used of the coming glory, but that the Greek word so translated is always used in this sense. It is most important that we should grasp this threefold idea of our salvation. It consists in Christ imputed as righteousness, imparted as sanctification, implanted as glorification. I was saved in the essential fact of my being, my spirit, when in answer to my faith Christ was imputed to me as the righteousness of God. I am being saved in mind or consciousness as Christ through all the discipline of the present life is being imparted to me as sanctification. I shall be saved finally when my body shall be fashioned anew in the likeness of His glorious beauty, when Christ shall be implanted within me and manifest through me. Through the mediatorial work of Jesus righteousness is made mine, sanctification is being made mine, redemption in its perfection will yet be made mine.

If we are to pray we must answer the claims of these truths. How am I to answer the claims of righteousness ? By yielding myself to God as one alive from the dead. In proportion as I do that I am prepared for prayer. The dynamic of prayer is holiness, which is rectitude of character, and righteousness, which is rectitude of conduct. Rectitude of conduct can only grow out of rectitude of character. Rectitude of character is given to me potentially when Christ is imputed to me. My responsibility is that I yield myself as one alive from the dead to Jesus Christ for righteousness. How am I to respond to sanctification ? Sanctification is the imparting of Christ to me, grace for grace. That is to say, every grace which is in Him, is in Him for me, and my responsibility is that I appropriate day by day what He communicates in order that He may reproduce Himself in me. When in order that I may be more perfectly conformed to His image, the indwelling Christ calls me to some new duty, some new sacrifice, some new enterprise, I must answer with ready consent. If I do, prayer prevails. If I refuse, prayer becomes impossible.

Finally, what response can I make to-day to the future tense of my life in Christ? Dr. James Denney in his book on Thessalonians says, "The attitude of expectation is the bloom, as it were, of the Christian character. Without it there is something lacking. The Christian who does not look onward and upward wants one mark of perfection. This is in all probability the point on which we should find ourselves most from home in the atmosphere of the Christian Church. Not unbelievers only, but disciples as well, have practically ceased to think of the second advent. . . . Yet a truth so clearly a part of Scripture teaching cannot be neglected without loss." I believe that to be most important truth. We have been so afraid of being called otherworldly, that we have not cared even to sing hymns about heaven. It is a grave mistake. We have been so afraid that some one would name us star-gazers, that we have abandoned all speech concerning the second advent. Yet the only light that we can ever shed upon the darkness of the world must be light beaming from the face lifted towards God's to-morrow. In the matter of prayer this is of supreme importance. To pray with prevailing power there must be the vision of the morning breaking in the Eastern sky. It is the man who sees the coming glory who knows what it is to put blood and sacrifice into the business of establishing that Kingdom here. In order to pray prevailingly, I must live in the power of the hope that maketh not

ashamed, having my face ever lifted towards the
light while I yet look at the sorrow around me,
and serve diligently the will of my King.

Once again, there must be response to the
Spirit. I am not now proposing to deal with the
whole of the Spirit's work, but with that whereby
He creates intercession. I would suggest three
words as helpful in following the line of thought.
They are, interpretation, consciousness, desire.
The Spirit of God indwelling interprets. His
interpretation creates a consciousness. That consciousness creates a desire, and that is prayer.

> Prayer is the soul's sincere desire
> Uttered or unexpressed ;
> The motion of a hidden fire
> That trembles in the breast.

The indwelling Spirit knows the will of God and
interprets it to the soul in whom He abides.
This He does by unveiling Christ, who is the
revelation of the will of God to me. As He was
the Word of God incarnate, He was the will of
God incarnate. I come to Him that I may see
what is God's will for myself and for all men ;
that I may understand what is God's purpose
concerning the whole world. As we look out
upon the movements of the hour and upon all
the facts of life, the indwelling Spirit sets them
in relation to the will of God, and a keen consciousness is born within us of the failure in the
midst of which we live. Thus the Spirit makes
intercession in us with groaning which cannot be

uttered as He gives us this new consciousness of
the limitation and paralysis of all life without
God.] As the Spirit interprets to us the will of
God, He shows the disaster of being out of
harmony with that will. As the Spirit interprets
the will of God, therefore, He makes the soul
profoundly discontented with everything that is
contrary thereto, and this because of the soul's
supreme content with the good and perfect and
acceptable will of God. That is what the apostle
meant when he wrote, " The whole creation
groaneth and travaileth in pain together until
now. And not only so, but ourselves also, which
have the first-fruits of the Spirit, even we ourselves groan within ourselves." Faber sang this
sublime and overwhelming truth in simplest
words, " Earth's sorrows are most keenly felt in
heaven." The heavenly people are, therefore,
those who most acutely feel earth's sorrows and
are able to enter into fellowship with God in
prayer for the winning of the victories of His
love. Following consciousness of discontent is
that of desire for the coming of the Kingdom, for
the setting up of the will of God, which means
the healing of wounds and the breaking of chains.

To that work of the indwelling Spirit there
must be ready response " Quench not the Spirit."
When the Spirit interprets the will of God for
life, for home, for city, for nation, we must listen
to no other philosophy, be seduced by no other
ideal. As the glories of that Kingdom flame
and flash before us, we must never be turned

aside by the glamour of the things of the world, the flesh and the devil. Answer the Spirit. Let Him teach. Let Him show the vision. Believe the Spirit. "Quench not the Spirit."

But more, infinitely more. When the Spirit revealing the will of God for the world creates in the heart a great pain and a great discontent, do not let us check it. That is what Christian men and women, alas, are too constantly doing. When the story of the sin and sorrow of humanity is told, they close their ears and are not willing to share in the pain. That is to grieve the Spirit indeed. We ought to hear. We ought to know. We ought to be ready to bring the new sensitiveness of our Christian life into close touch with the world's agony until we feel its pain as our very own. The Spirit desires that we should know its sorrow. His work is to interpret to us the meaning of the sob and sigh and the agony of the world. When we feel that, there will spring out of our life a new desire which will drive us to prayer that God's Kingdom may come, and to self-sacrificing service without which such prayer is blasphemy. Thus we shall begin to sob with God and to God, in our sense of the world's sorrow. Out of such prayer the toil and travail come which bring the Kingdom in.

Thus it will be seen that preparation for prayer is no slight, spasmodic process. It is the supreme matter of life. Yet, thank God, we can, if we will, respond to this revelation, mediation and inspiration so as to pray with prevailing power.

THE PLANE OF PRAYER
(a) The Purpose of God

V

THE PLANE OF PRAYER
(a) The Purpose of God

WE now come to the consideration of the plane upon which prayer is operative, the subjects concerning which we have authority to pray. This plane is revealed in the pattern prayer as it occurs in the Manifesto of the King.

Some few preliminary words are necessary. I find there are some who object to the use of this prayer by Christian people. I have for a long time been endeavoring quite honestly to understand the position of such, and I think the objections which they raise may be briefly stated. First, there are those who do not use this prayer because they say its petition for forgiveness is not the Christian petition. They affirm that we have no need now to ask for the forgiveness of our debts on the basis of having forgiven our debtors. My answer to such is that they certainly do not understand the real meaning of this prayer, or else they do not understand themselves. Their objection, however, will best be dealt with when we come to the more particular consideration of that petition in the second part of the prayer. Others do not use the prayer because they declare they have no sins to confess or ask forgiveness for. Again, I can only say all such either do not understand the meaning of the words "debts" and "debtors," or else they are wofully self-deceived. Perhaps the most serious and intelligent objection is that of those who say that this prayer was part of the Messianic Manifesto, that it had to do with Christ's teaching regarding the Kingdom, and that therefore it is the prayer of the Kingdom and not the prayer of the Church. I carefully distinguished between the Kingdom of God, the Kingdom of heaven, and the Church of Jesus Christ, but I do not propose to discuss these distinctions now. I recognize that the Church is, according to New Testament teaching, a separate entity having as its final purpose a vocation in the ages to come in the heavenly places. While that is perfectly true and should never be forgotten, indeed must not be forgotten, it is also true that for the present hour all the principles of the Kingdom are committed to the Church to be realized within the Church and through the Church manifested to the world. Consequently everything that Jesus said in His Manifesto concerning the Kingdom does apply to the Church. As a matter of fact that Manifesto of the King does not apply at all to the outside world. For the present day its only application is to the Church. That is another point which I do not propose now to elaborate. It is sufficient for the present purpose to say that to attempt to bring about the conditions described in the great Manifesto of the King among the vast unregenerate masses of the people is inevitably to be doomed to disappointment. The things which Jesus said to His disciples, I maintain, are only applicable to those who are in His Kingdom and subject to His rule. That Manifesto was the enunciation of the ethic of the Kingdom which no man can accept or obey while he is still in rebellion against the King Himself. That is a broad and hurried statement; but if it be accepted it will be seen that in the Church which for this age, according to the purpose of Jesus, embodies the principles of the Kingdom and manifests them in the world this prayer has its rightful place. The supreme answer to objections to its use will be found in an understanding of the prayer itself. In proportion as we really comprehend its intention, its spaciousness, its magnificence we shall be compelled to use it. There can be no escape from the use of it for such as are submitted to the reign and Lordship of Jesus Christ and are in sympathy with Him in His desires for the world.

Yet another word by way of introduction. It has been affirmed and correctly so, that this is not a new prayer. Its every petition is to be found in the Talmudic writings. We are not familiar with these writings, and so the different petitions of the prayer are known to us only through the Christian use of them. There can be little doubt, however, that the men who heard the Master when He first gave them the prayer were familiar with all its petitions. In all probability they had used them constantly in

their worship from childhood up. Now, while
that is true, it is also true that the prayer was
absolutely new as it came from the lips of Jesus.
He gathered together the things with which they
were most familiar and placed them in such perfect relation to each other as to reveal as never
before the whole plane of prayer. To pray that
prayer intelligently is to have nothing else to
pray for.) It may be broken up, each petition
may be taken separately and expressed in other
ways, but in itself it is inclusive and exhaustive.
The Jewish Rabbis taught the people what were
known as "index prayers." These consisted of a
collection of brief sentences, each one of which
suggested a subject of prayer. One of their
habits of praying was to take such an index
prayer, recite one petition at a time, and elaborate it in the presence of God by carrying out its
thought; and endeavouring to express its full in-
tent. In that sense the Lord's prayer also is an
"index prayer." There can be no desire of the
human heart which is inspired of the Holy Spirit,
no petition presented to the throne of the Father
but that it is included in this prayer. The King
wove together all the essential petitions which lay
scattered over the field of human praying into
one perfect whole which covers the ground and
reveals to men for evermore the plane upon
which they may pray. Thus it is a pattern
prayer.

Turning to examination I shall ask you first of
all to notice its structure. I am so increasingly

convinced of the value of eye-gate that I want
you to look at the prayer in this form —

> Our Father which art in the heavens,
> Thy name be hallowed,
> Thy Kingdom come,
> Thy will be done
>   as in heaven so on earth.
> Give us this day our daily bread.
>   And
> Forgive us our debts as we also have
>   forgiven our debtors.
>   And
> Lead us not into temptation, but deliver us
>   from evil.

You will notice first that the doxology with
which the prayer closes is omitted. I suppose
most of us felt some kind of a pang when, taking
up the Revised Version, we found it absent. Yet
there can be no question as to the accuracy of the
omission. Even so conservative and scholarly an
expositor as Hengstenberg says concerning this
doxology that there is no doubt that it ought to
be omitted. He goes on to say that so perfect an
ending to the prayer had better be retained and
made perpetual use of. I have great sympathy
with the sentiment of that view, but it cannot be
permitted in any strict dealing with the Scripture. Personally I should never think of using
the prayer without the doxology, but I should
ever remember that the doxology was the answer
of man to the inspired prayer rather than a part
thereof. Now let us notice the structure of the
prayer as I have attempted to set it out. The
whole is introduced by an invocation —

Our Father which art in the heavens.

This invocation prepares the way not for the first three petitions only, but for the whole prayer. It is a reverent form of address, and by the use of it we are brought into the presence of the revealed Father.

Beyond the invocation the prayer falls into two parts. The first consists of three petitions with a qualifying phrase; the second consists of three petitions.

Let us look at the first three petitions, and the relation to them of the qualifying phrase.

Thy name be hallowed,
Thy Kingdom come,
Thy will be done
as in heaven so on earth.

It is not " Thy will be done on earth as it is in heaven." The final phrase refers to all the petitions, and not merely to the last. The first half of the prayer is therefore one in which we ask that God's name may be hallowed, that His Kingdom may come, that His will may be done on this earth as in heaven. The three petitions form one whole petition. They mark stages in development. The first stage is the hallowing of the Name. That is followed necessarily by the crowning of the King and the coming of the Kingdom. When the King is crowned and the Kingdom established it is demonstrated amongst men by the doing of the will of the King by those who have hallowed His Name, and in whom the Kingdom

is established. Thus the first half of the prayer
has to do wholly with the purposes of God for
the world. In some senses all my need is included in this first half. It is not expressed there.
The only thing expressed is the passion for the
gaining of God's victory.

In the second half we have again three petitions —

> Give us this day our daily bread.
> And
> Forgive us our debts, as we also
> have forgiven our debtors.
> And
> Bring us not into temptation, but
> deliver us from evil.

Notice the position of the "and" in this setting,
how it links the second petition with the first, and
the third with the second. Notice also carefully
that the phrase "Bring us not into temptation,
but deliver us from evil," is not two petitions but
one. We are constantly hearing of the seven petitions of the Lord's prayer. There are only six,
and to make two petitions of the sixth is to create
difficulties which cannot be explained. Taken as
one it is a perfect petition, expressive at once of
the soul's caution and the soul's courage.

These last three petitions have to do wholly
with human and temporal needs as the three first
have to do with the Divine and eternal interests.
We shall not pray these last three petitions when
we get to heaven. I think the saints there are
still praying the first three. I think, moreover,
that they will continue to pray them until the

work is perfected, and that is not yet. Before turning to fuller consideration of the first half of this wonderful prayer, it is important to notice that in its very structure there is teaching. Jesus said, "Seek ye first His Kingdom, and His right-eousness; and all these things shall be added unto you." That was His order for life. It is also His order for prayer. Prayer only fulfills the Master's ideal when it begins with the interests of God and follows with the needs of man. I am afraid that order rebukes very much of our pray-ing. Are we not all more or less in danger of praying first for all our own needs, and then in a closing sentence or two for the coming of the Kingdom of God? Christ in the form of this prayer teaches us that our first business in prayer is to seek with God for His victory in the world; that the deepest purpose of prayer is not that we may obtain what we need, but that God should gain that which glorifies His name. Passion for the establishment of the Kingdom of God in the world is the deepest note in prayer.

Now let us take the first part of the prayer and look at it a little more closely. We find that the word "heaven" occurs both in the invocation and in the qualifying phrase. Its recurrence arrests our attention, and at once we are conscious of a light and glory irradiating these first petitions. We pause therefore to inquire what this word is and what it suggests. We shall find that it is used in the New Testament with reference to three distinct spheres, or places, or regions, whichever word may define most accurately the indefinable spaces beyond our earth. It is used first of the atmosphere. "Behold the birds of the heaven." It is also used of the stellar spaces stretching far beyond the atmosphere. "I will show wonders in the heavens." It is used of still another region, of the dwelling place of other beings, of the place where the glory of the infinite God is supremely manifest. "I knew a man in Christ, fourteen years ago (whether in the body, I know not; or whether out of the body, I know not; God knoweth), such a one caught up even to the third heaven." We cannot place these ideas in relation to space because we know so little concerning it. There is a sense in which the third heaven enwraps and permeates the second and the first. All I want now to make clear is that the word "heaven" is used with a threefold significance, and while poets and dreamers speak of a "seventh heaven," the Bible speaks only of a third. The word "heaven" therefore stands for the atmosphere, the stellar spaces, and finally the dwelling place of saints and angels.

Yet another note upon this word. It is written sometimes in the singular and sometimes in the plural and our translations do not show the difference uniformly. When in the singular it refers to one or other of these heavens; when in the plural it may refer to two or even three. The context or evident sense of the passage must decide which of three. "The day of the Lord will come as a thief; in the which the heavens shall

pass away with a great noise." The reference
here is evidently to the atmospheric and the stellar
spaces, the two first heavens.   Stephen when dying exclaimed, "Behold, I see the heavens opened,
and the Son of Man standing on the right hand
of God."   He saw beyond the atmosphere, and
beyond the stellar spaces into that place where
God's glory is supremely manifest and the spirits
of just men are.

In the invocation the word " heaven " is plural.
In the qualifying phrase at the close of the first
three petitions it is singular.   " Our Father which
art in the heavens."   Which of them ?   All of
them.   Thus there is found at the portal of the
prayer the doctrine of the transcendence and im-
manence of God.   Your thought cannot carry you
so far away as to escape Him ; and yet where you
are at this moment, "Closer is He than breathing,
and nearer than hands and feet."   Let us try to
realize this by the simplest of simple diagrams.

SAINTS AND SERAPHIM

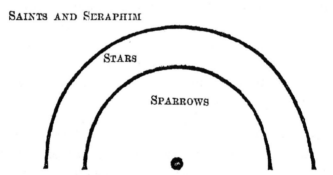

Taking that dot as centre I sweep a segment of
a circle round it to represent the atmosphere

which extends for forty miles outward from the
earth. That is the first heaven of the New Testament. Beyond that I sweep a larger segment
representing the vast stellar spaces. That is the
second heaven. Beyond that again is the third
heaven. In the first circle I write the word "sparrows"; in the next "stars," and in the next "saints
and seraphim." We are here on this little earth,
and having seen the revelation of the Father and
yielded to the mediation of the Son, and answered
the inspiration of the Spirit we are prepared for
prayer. Jesus now says to us, "After this manner therefore pray ye; Our Father which art in
the heavens." That is to say that the God who
hears prayer is in all the heavens. That great and
gracious fact is proven by other words of the Divine oracles. He is in the first heaven, the atmosphere; "Are not two sparrows sold for a
farthing? and not one of them shall fall on the
ground without your Father." Let us most ear-
nestly guard against spoiling the thought in that
quotation by adding to it a single word. It is
constantly rendered, "not one of them shall fall
on the ground without your Father's *knowledge.*"
Jesus did not say that. It would have been a
beautiful thing to say, but what He said was finer
far, "not one of them shall fall on the ground
without your Father." He not only watches from
afar the sparrow's fall, but He holds it dying.
The frailest bird dying of summer heat or winter
cold is not alone. It dies in the company of God.
And what of the stars of the second heaven?

" By the greatness of His might, and for that He
is strong in power, not one is lacking." "Up-
holding all things by the word of His power."
And what of the saints and seraphim? They veil
their faces in the presence of His glory, and do
His will in the consciousness of His nearness.

Thus as I begin to pray according to the pattern
which the Lord gives me, I find at the portal of
my prayer a doctrine of God which assures me
that nothing is beyond His reach, and nothing is
too small for His presence and attention. Oh,
the infinite comfort of it! Mother, praying for
your boy at the other side of the world, think of
it! Your Father is with him there. He is as near
to him as He is to you. Jesus did not say, Our
Father who is away off in some distant heaven far
removed from us; but rather, Our Father who art
in all the heavens; close at hand so that the least
whisper reaches Him, far away so that nothing
can escape Him.

Coming to the phrase with which these petitions
end we find that the word " heaven " is singular.
Now, while I do not mean to suggest that God's
will is not done in the atmosphere or in the stellar
spaces, I think it is evident that Christ's use of the
singular at this point indicates the fact that His
special reference was to that heaven where God's
glorious presence is supremely manifest, and where
the one abiding law is the law of His will. Thus
when we pray this prayer we are asking that as
His name is hallowed by the saints and seraphim,
as His Kingdom is established among them, and

as His will is the one and only law of all their activity, so on this earth His name may be hallowed,
His Kingdom come, and His will be done.   It is a
prayer that the order of heaven may be established
on earth.   When Jesus uttered these words and
gave them to His disciples as a pattern of prayer,
He of course knew perfectly that order of the third
heaven.   Indeed His vision and perfect knowledge
of that heavenly order were the inspiration of His
desire as He stood among the sin and sorrow of
this world.   As we interpret the prayer through
the One who gave it to us, it becomes an inspiration making us desire to know the order of the
third heaven.   Can we know anything of that
order other than speculatively ?   If there is one
thing concerning which no man ever ought to
speculate, it is heaven.   We have suffered terribly
in our ideas of heaven from grotesque imagination
concerning it.   I remember as boy that heaven
was to me a place where the saints sat on thrones
forever and ever wearing white robes and having
harps in their hands.   It was suggestive of deadly
monotony and far from attractive.   Such is not
the meaning of heaven.   Jesus did not want us to
pray that an order of that kind should be set up
on earth.   He was Himself a revelation to man
of the heavenly order.   Of the four evangelists
John is the one who interprets to us most perfectly
Christ as the Word of God out of heaven.   The
word "heaven" in John's Gospel is never plural,
and it always has reference to the third heaven.
The key words of John's writings are love, light,

life. "God is love," "God is light," "God is life."
These are three of the simplest words, and yet in
all human speech there are none sublimer. These
words perfectly portray the order obtaining in the
heaven of God. Grant me these three words with
all they suggest, and I care nothing about robes
and harps and thrones. There may be all these
things and will be, only do not let us forget that
all that we know of earth's beauties and splen-
dours are not worthy to be compared with the
grace and glory yet to be revealed.

In the third heaven love is the satisfactory impulse of everything. Light is the perfect intelligence in which all the inhabitants act. Life is
the sufficient power by which they walk in light
answering love. Love is impulse. Light is intelligence. Life is energy. The contrast between
the order of the third heaven and that obtaining
on earth to-day is at once manifest. No one is
prepared to affirm that love is the final reason of
all the activity of the world to-day. Christ says,
Pray that it may become so. Men do not walk
in perfect light even when it flashes upon their
pathway, for, as in the days of Christ so still,
men love darkness rather than light, for their
works are evil. Christ says, "Pray that men
may come to love light, and walk in it." And
yet men have not life sufficient to do the highest
and the best even when they know it. Toiler for
God, in your specific service you know what it is
to be weary. Do you know what weariness is?
It is the touch of death. Press your toil a little

further, a little too far, and all the weary wheels
stand still, and your eye sees no light, and your
heart can no longer love. That is the condition
of man in the world to-day. In God's third
heaven everything is different. Love is the reason of devotion and worship. Love is the inspiration of giving and receiving. Love is the impulse of revelation and explanation. Every move-
ment of the wing of the cherubim and every
note of the song of the seraphim are alike love-
impulsed. In heaven when love impulses light
falls upon the pathway, and mistakes are never
made through ignorance. There as in answer to
love the inhabitants serve in perfect light; they
are never weary for theirs is endless life. Jesus
said, Pray that all this may be so also on this
earth. Think what it would mean, what it will
mean for the world when that prayer is answered,
when "love" is the only reason, and "light" is
perfect intelligence, and "life" is sufficient power
for all accomplishment.

Can that prayer be answered? Will it be answered? The first reply to such a question is
that Jesus never taught men to utter vain prayers.
The fact that He gave us this prayer is enough
to make us offer it in the midst of the world's sin
and sorrow and sighing, knowing that because He
taught us so to pray the answer is bound to come.
And yet there is another and profounder argument for the reasonableness of this prayer, and
that is Christ Himself. Once in the history of
the world that for which the prayer asks has been

perfectly realized. Once the world saw, though it did not understand it, the heavenly order. It was manifest when He, who taught us to pray, tabernacled amongst men. Studying the life of Jesus as we have it in the fourfold Gospel, it is perfectly evident that wherever and whenever we find Him the one reason of His being, or doing, or saying anything is love. He was perfectly and wholly impulsed by love. This is true not only of His words and acts most evidently tender, but also of the severe things He said and did. Some of these were terrible indeed, scorching and startling men. On one occasion He looked into the faces of the rulers of His people and said, "Woe unto you, Scribes and Pharisees, hypocrites"; and it is impossible to read these words without being conscious that there was a note of terror in the voice of Jesus when He cried "Woe." Was that love? Yes, let Him finish His sentence, "for ye devour widows' houses." Love for the oppressed creates anger with the oppressor for evermore. Is there any phrase more startling than "the wrath of the *Lamb*"? I think that if we had desired to describe wrath figuratively we should have written, the wrath of the "lion," but therein we should have failed. It is the wrath of the Lamb which is terrible, the wrath of One whose very heart and nature are love and gentleness. Wrath kindled by love is the fiercest flame that burns.

It is also true that in all the life of Jesus there was manifest the light of a perfectly informed intelligence. He never hesitated. He was never perplexed. He never took counsel even with His own disciples. He consulted neither Conventions, Conferences, nor Committees. Ah, some one acquainted with the New Testament challenges that statement, and suggests that at least upon one occasion He called His disciples into Consultation. There was a day on which He asked one of them what was to be done to feed the multitude: but continue the story and you will read " *This He said to prove him:* for He Himself knew what He would do." Thus on the only occasion when it is ever suggested that He took counsel with His disciples the evangelist is careful to tell us that it was not that He might get advice, but in order that He might teach them something. He ever passed straight onward, and that perpetually on an illuminated pathway. Answering love He saw His way before Him and without hesitation walked in it.

But, it will be said it was not true of Him that He had endless life—He died. Let me say first in answer to such an objection, that the life of Jesus was always sufficient for the doing of the will of God, and even though He knew in sympathy with us the heavy weariness which follows toil, He was never weary while God-appointed service waited for Him. And yet again, He had the power of endless life as witness His own strange words, " I lay down My life, that I may take it again. No one taketh it away from Me, but I lay it down of Myself. I have power to lay it down, and I have power to take it again. This commandment received I from My Father." Death in the case of every other man is a fact from which He cannot escape. Death in the case of Jesus was an act in the mystery of which He was yet the supreme Lord and Master. He died and rose again in fulfillment of these wonderful words. Once in human history the heavenly order has been seen in a Man who answered love and walked in light, and had such life as enabled Him to die and to live again, and so doing to fling up a highway out of death for all such as trust and follow Him.

But what did the world do with this Revealer? The story is that of the world's final tragedy. Hatred murdered love. Darkness put out light. Death conquered life.

The Cross was man's answer to this prayer. But again, the Cross was God's answer to this prayer. Put both things together, or let us hear them put together by Peter in the first message delivered after Pentecost. "Him, being delivered up by the determinate counsel and foreknowledge of God, ye by the hand of lawless men did crucify and slay." Man's attitude towards the revelation of the heavenly order—" ye by the hand of lawless men did crucify and slay," God's activity in the midst of the mystery of death—" delivered up by the determinate counsel and foreknowledge of God." Over against the lawlessness of man's murder the deliberate counsel of God is operative, and thus the very Cross which marks man's refusal of the Kingdom becomes the means by which that Kingdom is yet to be set up.

When thus we observe the Man who taught us this prayer and come to understand that He embodied in His own life the principles He bids us seek, and when we know that by His Cross He made it possible for every man to come after Him, to answer "love," and to walk in "light" in the power of "life," then we pray the first part of this prayer as never before, realizing that in the name and merit and might of Him who taught us so to pray its final answer must come.

Thus the pattern prayer teaches us first that we must take the whole world into our praying, and that we must see clearly that the line of its redemption is that of return to conformity to the will of God, made possible by the life and death and resurrection of Him who taught us to pray—

> Our Father which art in the heavens,
> Thy name be hallowed,
> Thy Kingdom come,
> Thy will be done,
> as in heaven so on earth.
> Give us this day our daily bread.
> And
> Forgive us our debts, as we also
> have forgiven our debtors.
> And
> Lead us not into temptation,
> but deliver us from evil.

THE PLANE OF PRAYER
(b) The Pilgrimage of Man

" Give us this day our daily bread. And forgive us our debts, as we also have forgiven our debtors. And bring us not into temptation, but deliver us from the evil one."—MATTHEW 6 : 11-13.

VI

THE PLANE OF PRAYER

(b) The Pilgrimage of Man

WE now come to the second part of the pattern prayer. As the first part has to do with the interests of God, the second half deals with the pilgrimage of man; that is to say, it has to do with the needs of man in the days of his sojourn in this world. Its three petitions express the needs of these days of pilgrimage towards the Father's home. It will be impossible to use these petitions when we reach that home. They express our present need in the listening ear of God.

If these petitions be intelligently apprehended, it will be found that they cover the whole of our possible requirements. We may break up the petitions, we may give expression in the hours of communion with God to the detailed and specific need of which we are conscious, but we cannot pray for anything which is not included in these requests.

In previous chapters we have dealt with the threefold fact concerning God which Jesus has revealed. He is King, Father, Shepherd. In that order men come into relationship with Him. Having submitted to His Kingship, they find Him to be their Father. Then as they begin to walk along the pathway which His will appoints, they experience His care as a Shepherd.

The part of the prayer at which we are now to look is the cry of children-subjects, asking for the privileges of the flock, for the care of the one great Shepherd. In it there are three petitions —

> Give us this day our daily bread.
> And
> Forgive us our debts, as we also
> have forgiven our debtors.
> And
> Bring us not into temptation, but deliver us
> from evil, or, from the evil one.

As we study these three petitions we shall find that in each of them three sets of forces with which we daily come in contact are recognized. Every man upon the pathway of his pilgrimage has to do every day with God, with man and with the devil. That fact may be expressed in other words. We may say that we have to do with the upper world, with the world about us, and with the under world of evil. Every day we who are children of God have necessarily some dealings with God; every day we are in contact with our fellow man; and I do not think any one will dispute with me when I declare that for the saint of God there is no day in which he or she has not something to do with the spirits of evil. The three worlds are present in every one of these petitions, but in each petition one realm is referred to with special emphasis. To take the first, "Give us this day our daily bread." That petition has to do preeminently with our relationship to God, our dependence upon Him; but we shall find recognized in it our relationship to our fellow man, and also our relationship to the spirits of evil. The preëminent note is our relationship to God. In the second petition, "Forgive us our debts as we also have forgiven our debtors," the principal emphasis is upon our relationship to our fellow men. The relationship to God is acknowledged and the relationship to the under world is evident. In the final petition, "Lead us not into temptation, but deliver us from evil," the principal emphasis is upon our relationship to the under world. Our relationship to God is also recognized and that to our fellow man is present.

When referring to the threefold fact of the heavenly order proceeding from the government of God we mentioned three words which are constantly repeated in the writings of John, "Life," "Light," and "Love." The first of these three petitions is a cry for sustenance to God as "Life." The second is a cry for rectitude to God as "Light." The last is a cry for victory to God as "Love." So that the threefold order, which we first are taught to pray may, be established in the world, is recognized when we continue to pray about our own personal and individual needs.

In the economy of Jesus Christ, prayer never loses sight of the infinite relationships and the

infinite values.   Herein is the test for our praying.   The moment prayer becomes request for
something purely for self which may be spent
upon personal lusts—or if you will have a milder
word, upon personal desires—then prayer is outside the will of God.   If I ask for sustenance it
must be in a petition which recognizes that real
life is related to the life of God.   If I ask for
rectitude it must be in a petition which recognizes rectitude as being in right relationship with
the light of God.   If I ask for succour, deliverance from the evil of the under world, it must be
in a petition which recognizes the tender love of
God manifesting itself supremely in its persistent
determination that I shall be delivered from evil.
So that all prayer is to be tested by its relationship to the infinite and eternal verities and values.

Let us now take the petitions one by one.   In
the first, "Give us this day our daily bread," we
have the threefold relationship.   First, it is a cry
to God as "Life" for sustenance.   There is also
recognized the relationship to man.   We cannot
begin to pray this prayer alone; we immediately
bring others with us into the place of prayer not
as to bodily presence but as to social interest.
That fact is true of the whole prayer, but specially
true of the first petition.   We have also the reference to the under world, because life fed with
daily bread is made strong against the solicita-
tion of the spirits of evil.   The principal emphasis is, however, upon our relation to God.
What then does this prayer mean, "Give us this

day our daily bread"? What is daily bread? What did our Lord mean we were to pray for at this point? Let us omit the word "daily" for the moment, and read "Give us this day our bread." Of what bread was He speaking? There are those who hold that this prayer simply has reference to the bread of the physical life, and there are thousands of people who use it only in that sense. There are other people, some of them gifted expositors of the Word of God, who hold that our Lord was not referring in any way to the physical bread but that this is wholly a spiritual prayer, and that therefore He is here referring to the sustenance of the spiritual life. I do not agree with either of these interpretations. I believe that when our Lord enjoins us to pray "Give us this day our bread" He means by the use of that word all that is necessary for the sustenance of the whole life, physical and spiritual. I believe that, because I never find Jesus dealing with men in compartments. He always dealt with the whole man, and when He taught us to pray this prayer He intended to teach us that we were perpetually to remember that we are absolutely dependent upon God for all that is necessary for the sustenance of our perfect and complete life. In Deuteronomy we read "Man doth not live by bread only, but by everything that proceedeth out of the mouth of the Lord." There, in these words He quoted in the midst of His own temptation, is His own recognition of the need of physical bread; and therein is His affirmation of the necessity for another bread, the Word proceeding out of the mouth of God. He Himself being the Word of God said, " I am the bread of life." When this petition is presented we are asking God to give us the sustenance necessary for our whole life, that necessary for our spiritual, and that necessary for our physical life. The latter is secondary but it is necessary, and is as much supplied by God as is the sustenance for the spiritual life. The first petition of our need is one in which we ask our Father to supply all that is necessary for our complete sustenance " Give us this day our bread."

I think that an understanding of the word " daily " will emphasize the accuracy of the interpretation I have given. There is difficulty here. As a matter of fact it is a word quite unknown in classical Greek, and it is a word which never occurs in the New Testament except at this point in Matthew 6 and in Luke 11 where our Lord took one or two petitions of the prayer and gave them to His disciples in answer to their request. It would be a fascinating theme for discussion and speculation as to where this word came from and what it really means. There are difficulties in tracing its root. You notice in the margin of the Revised Version this suggestion, " Give us this day our bread 'for the coming day.' " If you have noticed it, you have felt how curious a suggestion it is. I want to speak with all due carefulness, and I do not speak with-

out remembering that the marginal readings of
the Revised Version express the opinion of a majority of the translators. Nevertheless, I do not
think that the meaning of this word translated
"daily" is "the coming day." It is possible that
it came from a root which means "to-morrow";
but it is equally possible that it came from a root
implying "existence." It is not for me to go into
that particularly, but I do not hesitate to say my
own belief is that the latter is the root from
which this word "daily" came. "Give us this
day our bread of existence." Here is a piece of
speculation which you may accept or forget as
you like. I believe Jesus coined that word. You
cannot find it anywhere else. Then of course
there comes the question as to whether Jesus
spoke in Aramaic or Greek, and again we are face
to face with a question full of interest, and one
which I do not pretend to be able dogmatically
or finally to decide. Personally, I am of opinion
that the Gospel of Matthew was written in Greek,
and moreover that Jesus spoke a dialect of Greek
which was common at the time. It is interesting
to remember that Alford in his later editions
adopted that view, although in the earlier issues
of his work he had maintained the contrary. I
believe therefore that Jesus coined this word
"daily." What He told us to pray was, "Give
us to-day the bread we need for our existence";
that is, for our whole life, for the life which is
physical, for the life which is spiritual.

Passing from that discussion of the mere words

of the petition, let us think of its spiritual intention and meaning. We are to ask God every day
for what we need for the sustenance of our life.
There are two ways in which we neglect this petition. One way is that we pray it as though it
simply referred to the bread which feeds the body,
and forget that we need day by day to be fed by
God with the bread which supplies our spiritual
life. As God answers prayer for the bread of
the body so He answers prayer for the bread of
the spirit. How does God answer our prayer for
the bread of the body? Not by its miraculous
supply but by the gift of all such forces as are
necessary to enable us in coöperation with Himself to obtain for ourselves by labour the bread
we need. So with the spiritual bread. God does
not succour the spiritual life of any man on his
simple asking. Our spiritual life can only be
maintained and sustained as we in personal labour for the meat that endureth, meditate in His
Word day and night, feeding upon that Bread of
Life which came down out of heaven from God.

The other side of the lesson is that we are not
to forget in these days of incipient infidelity in
the Christian Church, that the table to which we
sit down every day is one He spreads. You have
heard the old story of the man who met a boy
in a village street carrying a loaf of bread. He
stopped the boy and asked him where he got the
loaf. "From the baker" was the reply. "Yes,
that is right, but where did he get it?" "He
made it," said the boy. "How did he make it?"

"With flour." "Where did he get his flour?"
"He ground the corn." "Where did he get his
corn from?" "He got it from the farmer."
"Yes, but where did the farmer get his corn?"
"Oh, from God," said the boy. "Then you got
your loaf from God!" We have been very much
like that boy. We have put God away back, behind the miller and the farmer, and have forgotten Him in the process. While we recognize the
need of the intermediation of all these instru-
ments, we are not to forget that it is God who
feeds us with food sufficient for body and soul.

> Back of the loaf is the snowy flour,
>   And back of the flour the mill;
> And back of the mill is the wheat, and the shower,
>   And the sun, and the Father's will.

This prayer brings me back every day as a dependent being to God, so that I have never any
right to pray this prayer if I am saying in my life
or by my actions, my own hand gets me this bread,
my own cunning, wit and wisdom provide for me
all I need of spiritual culture.

Notice the social character of this prayer. Have
you ever taken the trouble to write out the personal pronouns in the first person? If you have,
you will have discovered that there is not one in
the singular from beginning to end,—our, us, our,
us, our, we, our, us, us. They are all plural.
You cannot pray that prayer by yourself. You
cannot pray that short petition by yourself. I
remember a friend of mine, a deacon in one of

my former churches, on a certain Harvest Festival, came to me in my vestry and said—there was a deal of humour in him, there always is in saintly men,—" Well, Pastor, I suppose you won't use the Lord's Prayer to-night. We are going to thank Him for having supplied our daily bread, you won't ask Him for it ? " I replied that we should certainly use the Lord's Prayer that night, and that by so doing we should put ourselves into fellowship with all hungry souls. It is "us" and "our," not "me" and "mine." When we come into God's presence to ask for the supply of our own need we are to remember in loving sympathy the need of all those who have not yet received.

There is another suggestive fact about this prayer. There is only one nominative case in it. There are four objective and four possessive, but only one nominative. Do you not know that the nominative is the most popular case. Men like to talk in the first person singular, nominative ; but the nominative is only here once. "Forgive us our debts, as we also have forgiven our debtors." The only right in this prayer to be the subject of a sentence is that of the loving heart who forgives some other man. The prayer is a social prayer from beginning to end. The social quality is manifest in this first petition as it asks for sustenance not for "me and mine," but for "us and ours."

The relation to the under world is also recognized here. The man fed, physically and spiritually, is the man most likely to be strong against the solicitations of evil. That is why men are perfectly right when they tell us that we insult a hungry man when we offer him a tract about heaven. The first thing is to feed him, not simply because he clamours for bread, but because a fed man is one the devil does not like. It is the hungry man the devil attacks. If that be true physically, it is preëminently true spiritually. My brother see to it that when morning breaks you go to God for sustenance for your spiritual life. That will make you strong against the allurements of the devil. So many people turn out to face the temptations of the day spiritually unfed, spiritually hungry therefore, and they are attacked by all kinds of enticements of the enemy. It is the man fed by God, spiritually and physically who is likely to overcome in the hour of temptation.

In the second petition will you notice that the relation to God comes first. It always does even if the emphasis is not there. We are to ask forgiveness—this is the one petition to which most people object, and some attempt to escape from the prayer because of it. I am not particularly surprised that people criticise this petition more than any other. It is a very difficult one to pray, but let us remember that when Christ gave this prayer in His Manifesto, He commented only upon this petition. "For if ye forgive not men their trespasses, neither will your Father forgive your trespasses." So we must neither get away

from this petition, nor indulge in that criticism
which attempts to accommodate it to our own
failure. I had been speaking on this subject in
an American city, and afterwards received a letter
from a lady who was greatly perturbed because I
had put special emphasis upon the fact that Jesus
distinctly tells us we are to ask for forgiveness
when we have forgiven. She said that for years
she had changed the form of that petition for she
had been afraid of it, and had said, "Forgive us
our debts, and we will forgive our debtors." She
asked if I did not consider this to be sufficient. I
replied that God never does business on the basis
of a promissory note. We must get our forgiving done before we can ask for forgiveness. That
prayer is the prayer of the children of God, not
of the men outside. I do not go to the man outside who has never given himself to God and tell
him that if he will forgive everybody, God will
forgive him. God begins by forgiving us of His
own free grace without any condition. The un-
forgiven man can be forgiven now, without any
condition except that he believe on the Lord Jesus
Christ. He will blot out the sins of such like a
thick cloud. When that is done the soul enters
the Kingdom, and now Jesus superimposes upon
His own subject as the condition for forgiveness
that he should be forgiving. If we are unforgiving, in the necessity of the case God will not forgive us. There is no escape from it. Is not hatred
the most dastardly and heinous of all sins—
hatred, the thing that contradicts the essence of

God which is love ?   If in my heart there is bitterness and malice and revengefulness what is the
use of confessing other sins and expecting to be forgiven, nursing the while the most damnable sin ?
We who are children of God, subjects of the King,
flock of the Shepherd, cannot be forgiven unless
we forgive, for our refusal to forgive is the deepest
and worst sin of all.   I speak with such emphasis
because I think the Church of Jesus Christ is
cursed by an unforgiving spirit.   Men and women
are sitting down at the table of the Lord who do
not speak to each other.   We are unforgiving in
our theological controversies.   The sin for which
Moses was excluded from the earthly promised
land was that " He spake unadvisedly with his
lips," he manifested a provoked spirit in a righteous cause.   A righteous cause, but an angry, unforgiving man ; and God shut him out of the
land of earthly promise.   For evermore Jesus
Christ is saying to us every day, "Come and have
your Father's forgiveness for trespasses, but do
not ask for that until you have forgiven the man
who has trespassed against you."   What is trespass ?   For notice, in the actual text our Lord
used the words " Debt" and " debtors " and in
the exposition which follows, He used the word
"trespasses."   What   then   is   debt, trespass ?
There is a common quality in our Master's use of
the two words which helps us to understand it.
Trespass is intentional error, or willful transgres-
sion.   Trench has said the word means falling
where one should have stood upright, whether

one could help it or not. There of course arises
the whole question of sin and of what sin is. We
still believe that the whole meaning of the New
Testament evangel is that a man need not sin
willfully, but we still maintain that so long as we
walk the pathway of the earthly pilgrimage, in
comparison with God's high ideal we are as tres-
passers, coming short, so that of our best service
we have to say "we are unprofitable servants."

I pity the man who tells me he cannot pray
this prayer because he never trespasses. I pity
him because of his dim comprehension of the real
meaning of holiness and of sin. To the man who
walks in light there is no day when he does not
find it necessary to confess his trespasses. Let
us not forget this flaming scorching word of the
Master, that we are not to ask for forgiveness
until we have forgiven. "If therefore thou art
offering thy gift at the altar, and there remem-
berest that thy brother hath aught against thee,
leave there thy gift before the altar, and go thy
way, first be reconciled to thy brother and then
come and offer thy gift." I wonder how many
people would have to stay away from church next
Sunday if they were true to this word. We had
better stay away, and get right with our brother
before we come to the altar. "If ye forgive not
men their trespasses, neither will your Father
forgive your trespasses." Loving forgiveness of
my brother is the condition upon which I, a child
of God, may ask His forgiveness.

What relation has all this to the underworld

of evil? When we forgive those who have
wronged us, we have gained the mightiest victory
possible over the devil. In that day when we
trampled on our pride and sacrificed what we
speak of as our rights, when we triumphed over
pride and lovingly forgave the man who had
sinned against us, we know we were conscious of
God as we had never been before, and we were
conscious of victory over the enemy as we had
never been. There is nothing God loves and the
devil hates more than a man who can forgive.

We come to the last of these petitions. "And
bring us not into temptation, but deliver us from
the evil one." "Bring us not into temptation,"
that is the language of the cautious heart, of the
man who recognizes how terrible an experience
temptation is. But there is something more important than that I should be delivered from
temptation, and that is that I should be delivered
from evil. If I can only be delivered from evil
by passing through temptation, then that I be
delivered from evil is the supreme matter. In
that remarkable passage in Luke just before the
Gethsemane experience and again just after it,
the Lord said to His disciples, "Pray that ye enter not into temptation." He was passing down
to temptation then. As I watch Him in Gethsemane I hear the echo of temptation, "Father,
if Thou be willing, remove this cup from Me;
nevertheless not My will, but Thine be done."
That is the echo of temptation. I have heard
that before. I heard the enemy say to Him long

ago in the wilderness, "There are the Kingdoms
of the world which you have come to possess.
Your pathway to them is one of suffering and
shame. Fall down and worship me and I will
give them to you. Get to your goal by a short
cut." Here is the old method. Be very afraid
of any easy method to anything. I hear it again
later on, not as before in the open attack of the
foe, but through the subtle word of friendship.
When Jesus at Cæsarea Philippi mentioned the
cross, Peter said, "Not that, Lord! That be far
from Thee. Keys, yes; crowning, yes; building, yes; but not the cross!" Christ said to him,
"Get thee behind Me, Satan: thou art a stumbling-
block unto Me; for thou mindest not the things
of God, but the things of men." In the garden
of Gethsemane the devil comes no longer in open
attack, no longer in the guise of a friend, but in
the shrinking of His own soul. "If Thou be
willing, remove this cup from Me." Therein is
the philosophy of this petition, "Bring us not
into temptation." We are to be afraid of temptation. We are not to be foolhardy, treating it
as of no account. We are to shrink in its presence with that cautiousness which makes for
courage. But the more important thing is that
we should be delivered perfectly from evil.
"Bring us not into temptation, but deliver us
from evil." That is to be my prayer every day
to God who governs in hell as well as in heaven.
Recognition of the force of temptation and its
subtlety will make me pray, "Bring me not into

temptation," but the deepest passion of my whole life will be—"deliver me from evil."

What relation to other men is suggested in this last petition? Peter writing to Christian people said, "Be sober, be watchful: your adversary the devil, as a roaring lion, walketh about, seeking whom he may devour." Why were they to be sober and watchful? "Knowing that the same sufferings are accomplished in your brethren who are in the world." Let the light of that fall upon this petition. When we are face to face with the evil one and with temptation, we are not fighting a lonely battle, we are part of a great host. Our brethren are being tried also. If we win, they win in a greater measure. If we lose, we shall halt the whole battle and retard the final victory. I sometimes think if we could say this to young people as it ought to be said we might help them. Are you fighting against temptation? Remember it is not a lonely battle you are fighting, you are part of a great host. If you lose, if you are beaten, if the enemy overcomes you, the whole army of God is halted in its onward march. If you win, you hasten the coming of the Kingdom. The same sufferings are being accomplished in your brethren. Upon this stress and strife of the saints depends the hastening or retarding of the Day of God. So we are to pray together "Bring us not into temptation, but deliver us from evil." We fear the process, but there is a deeper passion than the passion for escape from testing, it is the pas-

sion for deliverance from evil.   That is the great
and final thing.

In conclusion, let it be noted that He who
taught the prayer has in its second half, as in the
first, guaranteed the answer.   Am I to pray for
the bread of life ?   He bends over me and says,
" I am the Bread of Life."   Am I to pray for
sustenance of the physical life ?   He whispers to
me, hear the tender promise, " All these things
shall be added unto you."   Am I to pray for forgiveness ?   Through His name is forgiveness
preached.   But how am I going to forgive the
man who has injured me ?   The Spirit of Jesus
is the spirit of forgiveness.   If I am yielded to
Him He is yielded to me.   If I give my whole
life to Him He will give His whole life to me.
If I have Jesus for my own I shall be able to forgive, so that He will answer this very prayer and
make possible its answer in the high court of
God's own judgment hall.   As to temptation,
" He was tempted in all points like as we are, sin
apart."   And " In that He Himself hath suffered
being tempted, He is able to succour them that
are tempted."

So in this pattern prayer He shows me what to
pray for as He opens before my astonished vision
the whole realm of prayer.   I end as I begin by
saying that if we can pray this prayer with spiritual intelligence and earnestness we pray all
prayer.

"*And when ye pray, ye shall not be as the hypocrites: for they love to stand and pray in the synagogues and in the corners of the streets, that they may be seen of men. Verily I say unto you, They have their reward. But thou, when thou prayest, enter into thine inner chamber, and having shut thy door, pray to thy Father which is in secret, and thy Father which seeth in secret shall recompense thee. And in praying use not vain repetitions, as the Gentiles do; for they think that they shall be heard for their much speaking. Be not therefore like unto them: for your Father knoweth what things ye have need of, before ye ask Him.*"—MATTHEW 6 : 5-8.

"*Again I say unto you, that if two of you shall agree on earth as touching anything that they shall ask, it shall be done for them of My Father which is in heaven. For where two or three are gathered together in My name, there am I in the midst of them.*"—MATTHEW 18 , 19, 20.

VII

THE PRACTICE OF PRAYER

THE subjects already considered are all preliminary to and necessary for the present one. God has made prayer possible to us through Jesus. We can pray prevailingly only as we respond to the truths which create the possibility. The sphere of prayer includes the coming of the Kingdom of God and the provision of all the need of the saints. Thus all these constitute an integral part of the subject of the practice of prayer. Prayer is only possible to the revealed Father through the mediating Son by the inspiring Spirit. Prayer is only a prevailing power as, in the life, the child of God is loyal to His Kingship, satisfied with His provision, conformed to His likeness. Moreover, it can only be operative within the sphere revealed in the pattern prayer.

All this being granted, we now come to the more technical consideration of this subject. It is necessary both in order to brevity and clearness that we should follow a process of elimination. The teaching of Jesus is so full of instruction concerning prayer that we do not propose to attempt even a survey of the whole field, but to confine ourselves to the words dealing with the two main lines of responsibility in this matter,

those namely, of the practice of prayer personally, and the practice of prayer collectively.

First, as to the former. " But thou, when thou
prayest, enter into thine inner chamber, and having shut thy door, pray to thy Father which is in
secret, and thy Father which seeth in secret shall
recompense thee." We are at once arrested by
the "but" with which the passage opens. It
makes us conscious of a background, of a contrast
which flung the actual words into clearer relief.
Immediately preceding Jesus had said, "Ye shall
not be as the hypocrites: for they love to stand
and pray in the synagogues and in the corners of
the streets, that they may be seen of men." Now
it is perfectly evident that our Lord did not mean
to say it was wrong to stand and pray in the syna-
gogue or at the corner of the street. That against
which He warned His disciples was the praying
which had as its deepest desire a wish to be seen
of men. He charged them to beware of the prayer
which obtrudes itself upon human notice. Mark
His gentle satire in this respect, "Verily I say
unto you, they have their reward." That is to
say, they pray to be seen of men, they are seen
of men. What they desire, they obtain. This is
the background. We are interested in the instructions to which these warnings gave rise.
" When thou prayest, enter into thine inner chamber, and having shut thy door, pray to thy Father
which is in secret." Thus Christ instructed His
disciples that in the life of each one of them there
must be a special place, a special time and a special

method, whereby in quietness and loneliness, every third person being excluded, each one should pray.

Then as to the latter, " If two of you shall agree on earth as touching anything they shall ask, it shall be done for them of My Father which is in heaven. For where two or three are gathered together in My name, there am I in the midst of them." As the first passage insisted upon loneliness, this provides for fellowship in prayer. It declares the conditions of the true prayer-meeting. The promise is indeed a spacious one. "If two of you shall agree on earth as touching anything that they shall ask, it shall be done for them." It is a somewhat curious thing that this promise is so perpetually misquoted by the addition of the words, "concerning My Kingdom." It may be said that this, of course, was what our Lord meant us to understand. I unhesitatingly reply that we have no right to imagine that He meant anything other than He said. To introduce these words is to put a limit upon prayer which He did not put. If it be objected that this is a dangerous doctrine, I reply that Christ clearly marked the limits of such agreement and such asking in the words, "For where two or three are gathered together in My name, there am I in the midst of them." The promise is not made to two or three persons who meet together, and ask simply upon the basis of their own desire. "Jesus in the midst" means Jesus enthroned, obeyed, consulted. Where He is enthroned, obeyed, consulted, the Spirit

creates desire, and prayer being in harmony
with the will of God, the answer is assured. We
must neither put false limitations upon this word
of the Master, nor must we imagine that there
are no limitations. According to Him, the limit
is not upon the things for which we may ask, but
upon our condition and the Spirit in which we ask.
Two or three of us may agree as to our desire for
certain things, and may ask for them, and never
receive them. The prayer-meeting must not be
based upon desire, but upon relationship to Christ.
If two or three of us are gathered together in His
name, under the dominion of His life, inspired by
His Spirit, and if in the hearts of those thus gathered there is created a common desire, then they
may ask and be assured of the answer.

These then are the two words of Jesus about
prayer which reveal the broad lines of its practice.
Firstly that we enter into an inner chamber, shut
the door, and pray alone; and secondly, that we
gather together two or three in His name and pray.
One man may pray alone, indeed he must do so
shutting out every other person ; but that does not
exhaust the practice of prayer. There must be
the prayer-meeting. It is not necessarily a large
gathering. The Master names the smallest number that can constitute a meeting—two. There
cannot be a meeting of one. Yet the larger number is not necessarily wrong. The indefiniteness
of His phrase " two or three " includes the possibility of the larger gathering. That which creates
the true prayer-meeting is the inspiration of saints

in communion with each other, because baptized by the Spirit into living communion with Christ.

Now for the most practical of words concerning each of these methods. As to the first, I desire to insist upon the necessity for the formation of very definite habits. The words of the Master could not be more emphatic than they are as to the necessity for separation, seclusion, and secrecy. An inner chamber and a shut door certainly mean that there must be in the life of every man or woman or child a place for retirement, a time for seclusion, an exercise of this high and holy privilege in absolute loneliness, when husband or wife, father or mother, brother or sister, son or daughter, is excluded. In all our busy life nothing is of more importance than that we should have some place peculiarly consecrated to prayer. The soul needs a Bethel. It may not be a place retained exclusively for prayer, but it should be a place to which at set times we may go and know that we shall be free from intrusion. For every minister of the Gospel this Bethel ought to be his study. I know how constantly we think of the study as the workroom, and rightly so. Woe be to the preacher of the Word who is not a workman. But the study ought to be at times the place where we may look into the face of God alone and hold personal communion with Him. This may sound like a plea for the private oratory of the Roman Catholic, and so it is in all its deepest spiritual intention. For the material trappings of crucifix, picture, or candle I care nothing, but

for the spiritual intention of lonely communion
with God in some set place, I care increasingly.
There is far more than seems in the place set
apart.   Those of us who preach the Word surely
know what it is to feel the ease of preaching in
the place with which one is perfectly familiar.
Familiarity enables forgetfulness of surroundings.
The "where" matters little.   The fact that there
is a place is of great importance.   To object to the
idea of locality is to imagine there was no meaning in the words of Jesus when He spoke of an
"inner chamber" and a "shut door."   To the
merchant, it may be his private office, locked at a
certain time for loneliness with God.   To the
mother it may be the quiet of her own room from
which for a little she is able to exclude all those
who serve under her in the maintenance of home.
It seems to me that if the watchers in the heavenly places observe the places of the sons of men
amid earth's conflict, those in which they are
most interested are the secret places where the
saints hold converse with God.   Until we find
some place of habitual loneliness made sacred,
not by material accessories, but by spiritual ac-
cess, we are not as strong as we might be, and we
have not formed the mightiest habit in the life of
prayer.   Then it is of equal importance that there
should be a special time for prayer.   I am perfectly
well aware of the answer that comes from thousands of toilers to-day.   This is a busy age.   Of
that there can be no denial, but if the age is too
busy to pray, so much the worse for the age; or

rather if in the age we are too busy to pray, so much the worse for our business. As to the time of prayer there can be no little doubt that for those who are able the "morning watch" is the finest. Yet I would urge none to be slave of the habit of another. If a proper regard for physical conditions makes it necessary for some over-wrought daughter of the King to rest in the morning hour, let her remember that she is not under law, but under grace. Then let there be no escape from the importance of time by declaring the brevity of the day, and the multiplication of positive duties. In fellowship with God the terms long or short ought to be cancelled. Five minutes with Him in which the soul is touched by the forces of eternity will mean a day full of spiritual vigour. God can do much in five minutes of man's time if no more can honestly be spared. He can do nothing in five minutes for the man who should give Him sixty, who but is slothful. Those who know the value of lonely fellowship with God, at the beginning of the day, know also how hot and restless is the day from which that time of communion has been absent. Again I say, cultivate that method of prayer which is most helpful, whether it be that of speaking aloud in loneliness, or of communing in stillness of heart and silence, whether standing or kneeling or sitting. No special attitude is insisted upon as necessary in the Word of God. The matter of supreme importance is that we discover the method of prayer which helps us most actually

to realize the presence of God and hold communion with Him. The place, the time, the
method, are matters concerning which there must
be individual choice and decision. The matter of
supreme importance is the cultivation of the habit
of prayer. I do not use the word habit carelessly.
Habits need to be formed whether they are good
or evil. With regard to prayer that which is at
first perhaps somewhat trying and difficult, becomes so much a part of the life as to be not
second nature, but first nature. In all these matters it is important to distinguish between the es-
sentials and the accidentals.

It would be disastrous if any should imagine
that these set times exhausted the practice of
personal prayer. Our Lord declared that " Men
ought always to pray, and not to faint," and that
is a very profound word. It is evident that His
conception of life is that if men pray they will
not faint, and conversely, if men do not pray
then will they faint. This word indicates the
fact that Jesus had a profound consciousness of
the pressure and strain of life. He did not think
it was a soothing softness through which men
glide. To Him life was indeed simple, but also
strenuous. He knew that men would be in danger of fainting underneath the burden and in the
midst of the battle. He knew also a power
which would prevent their fainting. " Men
ought always to pray, and not to faint." No
man will pray always who neglects the formation of the habit of regular prayer. The dis-

ciple who regularly observes a place and time and method will gradually find the habit learned in the secret place is binding also through all the public life. A confirmed habit of regular prayer will create regularity and constancy amidst all irregularities of time and place and method. Prayer in the secret place will create a spirit which will obtain in all public places. Gradually thoughts will become prayers, thoughts of absent friends will take wings and move upwards. Fellowship with God as an activity will issue in fellowship with God as an attitude. When this is so, anywhere, and at any moment, and in any method the spirit will speak its need in the listening ear of God. Our fathers used to speak of and practice ejaculatory prayer. It would be a great gain to all of us if we could learn again the method and practice it. It is a great mistake to imagine that in the midst of London's busy traffic one has to wait for the appointed place and hour and method. It is a great word in the " letter to the Hebrews " which declares that we " may find grace to help us in time of need." I have always felt that I should like to discover some idiom of my own language which would gather the thought of the Greek phrase, and I am not sure but that it is perfectly done by saying that the message declares we may find grace to help us " in the nick of time." The consciousness of this, however, can only be created as we are familiar with the secret place as a result of the set time and place and method.

So far we have dealt with only the practice of prayer in the individual life, with the inner chamber and the shut door, the special place, the special time and the special method, and with prayer flung out in sighs and sentences in the rush of every-day activity, in the abiding consciousness of God's attention and God's answer.

Turning to the habit of collective prayer, there is very much that might be said about the prayer-meeting. The prayer-meeting is a meeting for prayer. That is so obvious a statement as to appear unnecessary. Yet I do not hesitate to affirm that there is nothing the Church needs more at the present hour than to understand what a real prayer-meeting is. As we have already briefly said, the perfect ideal is set forth in the Master's words, " Where two or three are gathered together in My name, there am I in the midst of them." He was primarily declaring the ground upon which He had made His promise " If two of you shall agree on earth as touching anything that they shall ask, it shall be done for them." I am perfectly aware that these sacred words of our Lord open before our vision vaster reaches, and have more spacious meanings, but at the present time we consider them only in the first application which our Lord made of them. The first necessity then for the prayer-meeting is that those constituting it should be gathered " in His name." Two souls so gathered, each under His dominion—and the place is of no moment. The great word " where " is magnificent in its

breadth ; no longer in Jerusalem, no longer at
the temple, no longer in a mountain set apart, no
longer in a church or meeting-house or any other
special place only, but " where," in the home, in
the field, upon the sea, on the mountain, in the
great cathedral, in the mission-hall, they are
" gathered in the Name."   We do not catch the
thought if we say " two or three *met* together,"
" *assembled* together," no, they must be " gathered," and the great and only " Gatherer " is the
Lord Himself, acting to-day through the Holy
Spirit.   Then they must be gathered " in His
name," which does not merely mean that they
must be called Christians, but they must be
sharers of His nature, those who are living His
life, under the impulse of His love, in the illumination of His light.   When such souls are so
gathered you have the prayer-meeting.   A meeting for prayer is a meeting of two or three units,
hundreds, thousands, gathered, as we have said,
and who give themselves to prayer. I may be
asked if I would discountenance singing and the
exposition of scripture in prayer-meetings.   Well,
I should certainly have no singing in a prayer-
meeting, save the singing of some of the great
prayer hymns of the Church, in which she is
rich. I would have no other reading of the
Word of God save perhaps some passage indicat-
ing our responsibility in or re-stating the charter
of prayer.   In the true prayer-meeting there
should be no " waiting."   By that I do not mean
that it is necessary always for some one to be en-

gaging in audible prayer, but rather that the cessation of the sounding of a human voice ought
not to mean the cessation of prayer. During all
the silent pauses, every individual should be in
silent communion with God, bearing up quietly
some petitions which perhaps have already been
decided upon or named in the assembly. Yet on
the other hand there should be no "waiting" in
the sense of refusing to lead in audible prayer
when the Spirit guides. Elder waits for younger,
younger waits for elder; the Spirit waits for all,
and is grieved and hindered. In the true prayer-
meeting there should be preëminently the consciousness that the saints are gathered not only
"in His name," but because in His name, in His
real presence. Where that is so there will be
"waiting" only for direction by the Spirit. It
may be objected that this kind of prayer-meeting
would not be popular, yet surely it has not come
to this that any Christian soul should imagine
popularity to be the standard of success in the
Church of God.

This habit of collective prayer should not be
confined to meetings merely in connection with
the Church, that is, on the Church premises. It
may be cultivated in the home-life, and indeed
everywhere. As an illustration, let me suggest
that Christian women should turn their faculty
for social entertainment in this direction. Why
not have "At Homes" for prayer? At least,
they would have the advantage of definiteness,
and in that very minor sense would be infinitely

superior to many of the unhallowed crushes which characterize so-called social life to-day. Why not issue invitations upon this basis, that your friends should meet in your home to spend an afternoon in prayer. If the so-called friends would not accept the invitation, then surely you, as a Christian, are better without such friends. /It is the Church's friendship with people who do not want to pray, which blights the Church and blights the world./ The people in the ungodly suburb where your home is, may be, according to the canons of a worldly hour, preëminently respectable, but if they are not prepared to come to your home to talk with Christ, they are injuring you and you are injuring them by your continued friendship. Not only in the home life, but in all social intercourse, the saints should come together more for prayer. I go back in memory to the days when, as a lad at school in Cheltenham, I formed a friendship with one David Smith, a colporteur. His memory is fragrant still. On half-holidays I would accompany him to some of the villages lying among the Cotswold Hills. It was our custom, at his suggestion, to start half an hour earlier than was necessary to bring us in time for the meetings in order that on the way we might make a pause for prayer together. Some of the most hallowed memories of my heart to-day are of those meetings of two, one a young man loving his Lord, and the other a boy, opening his eyes towards the possibility of a life-work, pausing at some stile amid the fields and agree-

ing together to ask, asking and obtaining answers.
The glory of such meetings lies in the utter ab-
sence from them of constraint or compulsion of
any kind other than that of the presiding Lord.
In such a meeting one may pray as many times
as the heart prompts. One may stop without
elaborate finish, and commence again because in
another's prayer a new desire has been born in
one's own heart. I think we cannot tell how
much it would mean to the strength of the
Church if the saints of God cultivated the habit
of fellowship in prayer in small groups.

There are three notes of prevailing prayer of
which I want to speak briefly. First, definiteness, secondly, importunity, and thirdly, submission. There is nothing we need more in personal
prayer than to know what we want, and ask for
it. It is possible to waste the great opportunity
of prayer by indefiniteness. We may generalize
prayer until we vapourize it, and there is no virtue
left in it. It is a question whether ministers can
serve their churches in any better way than by
the simple habit of praying individually for the
flock of God committed to their care. During
the two years of my ministry at Westminster I
have passed from North to South and East to
West of my own country, and have twice visited
the States. I have gone nowhere during that
period without discovering the influence resulting
from the ministry of the man of God who built
that place, and more than thirty years ago passed
on into the light of the Father's home. The

question arises as to what in the life and work of
Samuel Martin created the influence which so
long abides. He was an eloquent preacher, truly,
and a man of saintly character, but perhaps the
greatest thing about him was the fact of his
definite praying. It was his habit to go into that
great building when the doors were shut, and to
pass from pew to pew praying for the people who
occupied them at the regular services of the
church. The same truth applies to our work in
the Sunday-school. There is no more sacred,
holy, or beautiful work than that of the teacher,
no work that needs clearer vision or more tender
heart. Our teachers will find great help from
the practice of definite prayer for their children.
Let them make the register of the scholar's names
a prayer-book in the highest sense of that word.
As every child in turn is born upon the heart,
there will be created a new power for influencing
those thus prayed for towards Christ Himself.

All this is equally true of the collective praying
of the saints. Prayer-meetings have too often
been killed by aimless, rudderless, anchorless
wanderings of such as seem to have no haven. It
would be a habit of great helpfulness if before
prayer the Church decided what it was about to
pray for. It is impossible to pray about everything in one prayer-meeting. One day in a York-
shire prayer-meeting there came a stranger who
did what many men are in the habit of doing—
God forgive them—he made a prayer. When he
had been talking twenty minutes, and no living

man ought to pray in a prayer-meeting above
five, and had been giving the Almighty information of which He had been in possession
long before the man was born, at last he said,
" And now, O Lord God, what more shall we say
unto Thee ? "   An old man who knew how to
pray audibly replied " Call Him 'Feyther,' mon,
and ax for summat."   This principle of definiteness is what we supremely need in individual and
collective praying.   Jesus did not say, " If you
will give God information for twenty minutes in
elegant language you may derive some benefit
therefrom." He said, " Ask, and receive " ; " seek,
and find " ; " knock, and it shall be opened."

The next note of prevailing prayer is that of
importunity.   In the eleventh and eighteenth
chapters of Luke are two parables which show
this necessity.   The one is a picture of a man who
obtained bread by knocking and by continuing
to knock.   The other is a picture of a woman who
got redress for her wrongs by worrying a judge.
Now Jesus was not teaching that God has to be
begged in order to obtain His favour, not that
He needs to be worried in order to persuade Him
to do right, but rather that it is necessary for our
sakes that there should be importunity.   The man
who asks and forgets does not really feel his need,
and therefore will not receive.   The man who
knocks and runs away will never receive the
beneficence of the One who alone can open the
door.   The men who know the real secret of
prayer knows the meaning also of importunity.

Epaphras agonized in prayer.   There must be definiteness, and then importunity.

But importunity must never degenerate into self-will.   There must also be submission.   Submission as to the form in which the answer shall come; submission as to the method of the answer ; submission as to the time of the answer.   It must not be forgotten that we cannot see the end from the beginning, cannot understand the ultimate meaning of our own petitions, but we are praying to One who does see the end from the beginning, and who is perfectly conscious of the issue of our petitions.   It may be that the things which to us seem most necessary would only prove a hindrance if they were granted.   The best answer to such prayer is ever the kindly love which refuses. Therefore there must be submission in all prevailing prayer.

Then as to the subjects of prayer.   We are warranted in praying for anything which is within the sphere of the will of God.   That statement is inclusive and exclusive.   It includes everything which in itself is right, and which forms part of my life and service according to the Divine plan.   It excludes everything which is wholly self-centred.   There is no doubt that prayer in the Spirit will mean the cessation of a great many petitions.   Many things after which we have most strenuously striven even in prayer, we shall be able to strive after no more if our life is responsive to all the facts which make prayer possible.   Petitions will be fewer, but they will

be more powerful. One illustration of exclusion
may be valuable, and yet in giving it let me first
say that I am speaking from my own experience
only. There may be no application of this illustration to any other. We must all be perfectly
persuaded in our own minds on such things.
If we have faith we must have it to ourselves before God. But to return. I cannot pray as I
once did about the weather. Who am I that I
should ask that any given day in the calendar
should be fine? I am always profoundly thank-
ful that although our friends across the ocean are
able to send us weather forecasts, they do not
send us weather. God still holds the government
in His own hand. The mother of a friend of
mine, a Baptist minister, told me why she had
ceased praying concerning this matter. For many
years at family worship she had been in the habit
of asking for a fine day for the Sunday-school
outing. When her boy was about ten years of
age he came to her on one such morning and said,
" Mother, I don't think you ought to ask God for
a fine day. Perhaps it would be a great deal better for the farmers to have it wet, and why
should it be fine just for our outing?" She replied that of course her petition was that if it
should be God's will it might be fine. The boy
then said, " Why don't you ask God to help you
to choose one of His fine days?" To me that is
the whole philosophy of praying. It is not an
arrangement by which we obtain things which
we personally desire. It is rather the provision

through which we seek to be brought into conformity with the will of God, and to obtain only the light which enables us to walk therein. Not that it is wrong to ask definitely, but it is always wise to carefully weigh our petitions as to whether or not they really recognize His sovereignty and wisdom. Charles Kingsley refused on one occasion to use the Archbishop's prayer for the cessation of rain. He recognized that the long downpour was sorely needed for sanitary conditions.

There are particular things about which we ought to pray, for which we are commanded to pray ; for all the saints, for the Word of God, for the Christian ministry, for all souls.

Jesus prayed for all the saints in that great intercessory prayer. Paul prayed for these as the letters of the imprisonment testify. What a heal ing of our denominational differences would result, if instead of perpetually discussing those differences we gave ourselves to prayer for each other.

Then we should pray for the Word of God, that it "may run and be glorified." Again how much more powerful such action would be than that of debating our differing interpretations of its meaning. Then for the ministry. If the Church would pray for the ministry instead of criticising it, there would be wonderful results. In this connection I should like to urge upon the Church that its special duty according to the teaching of the Lord is to pray that God will

thrust out into His harvest His own labourers.
I am sometimes asked to appeal to young men to
enter the ministry because there is a need of
them. My answer is that no man can choose to
become a minister—he must be sent. Therefore
we should pray as our Master taught us that the
Lord Himself will send. In this connection also,
it may be well to urge the importance of praying for those who have the sacred and awful
charge of training men for the exercise of their
ministry. Then moreover, we are to pray for
the men who are exercising the holy calling. I
once heard Dr. Berry give a charge to a young
minister. In the course of that charge he said to
the people, "You will get out of my young
brother what you expect, and you will expect
what you pray for." Then he used this homely
but forceful illustration. Said he, "We were
giving soup away lately to our poor people, and
had issued general instructions that the lads who
came to fetch the soup should bring with them a
vessel that should hold about two quarts. I was
at the soup-kitchen one day, and saw a boy about
ten years of age, ragged and dirty, but with eyes
that flashed fire, going into the soup-kitchen carrying a vessel that would hold at least three gal-
lons. We could not for shame put two quarts
into that." "Now," said Dr. Berry, " when you
come to hear your minister, do not bring a two-
quart measure !" Oh, what it is to preach to men
and women who have been praying for you.

Then we are charged to pray for all souls, the

sorrowing, the sighing, the sad, the sinning.
Moreover there is no small matter about which
we have not the right to pray. Anna Shipton
wrote a little book called *Tell Jesus*, being the
memorials of Emily Goss. It is the story of a
girl who told Jesus everything, from the trouble
of a tangle in a skein of wool to the joys of the
passing hours.

From this sacred service of prayer no saint of
God is excluded ; the youngest and the weakest
can pray. There are some of us who are excluded from certain lines of service because of
the pressure of life upon us, but no one of us is
excluded from prayer. There are saints of God
who for long, long years have been shut off from
all the activities of the Church, and even from the
worship of the sanctuary, but who, nevertheless,
have continued to labour together in prayer with
the whole fellowship of the saints. There comes
to me the thought of one woman who, to my
knowledge, since 1872 in this great babel of London, has been in perpetual pain, and yet in constant prayer. She is to-day a woman twisted
and distorted by suffering, and yet exhaling the
calm and strength of the secret of the Most
High. In 1872 she was a bed-ridden girl in the
North of London, praying that God would send
revival to the Church of which she was a member, and yet into which even then she never came.
She had read in the little paper called *Revival*,
which subsequently became *The Christian*, the
story of a work being done in Chicago among

ragged children by a man called Moody. She had never seen Moody, but putting that little paper under her pillow, she began to pray, "O Lord, send this man to our Church." She had no means of reaching him or communicating with him. He had already visited the country in 1867, and in 1872 he started again for a short trip with no intention of doing any work. Mr. Lessey, however, the pastor of the church of which this girl was a member, met him and asked him to preach for him. He consented, and after the evening service he asked those who would decide for Christ to rise, and hundreds did so. He was surprised, and imagined that his request had been misunderstood. He repeated it more clearly, and again the response was the same. Meetings were continued throughout the following ten days, and four hundred members were taken into the church. In telling me this story Moody said, "I wanted to know what this meant. I began making inquiries and never rested until I found a bed-ridden girl praying that God would bring me to that Church. He had heard her, and brought me over four thousand miles of land and sea in answer to her request." This story is told in the life of D. L. Moody by his son: but now let me continue it. That girl was a member of my church when I was pastor at New Court. She is still a member, still suffering, still confined to her own room. When in 1901 I was leaving England for America I went to see her. She said to me, " I want you to reach that birthday book." I did so and turning to February 5 I saw in the handwriting I knew so well, " *D. L. Moody, Psalm 91.*" Then Marianne Adlard said to me, " He wrote that for me when he came to see me in 1872, and I prayed for him every day till he went home to God." Continuing, she said, " Now, will you write your name on your birthday page, and let me pray for you until either you or I go home." I shall never forget writing my name in that book. To me the room was full of the Presence. I have often thought of that hour in the rush of busy life, in the place of toil and strain, and even yet by God's good grace I know that Marianne Adlard is praying for me, and it is for this reason that to her in sincere love and admiration I have dedicated this book. These are the labourers of force in the fields of God. It is the heroes and heroines who are out of sight, and who labour in prayer, who make it possible for those who are in sight to do their work and win. The force of it to such as are called upon to exercise the ministry can never be measured.

The personal word must again be forgiven. I never stand up in any assembly at home or abroad without knowing that three people nearer to me than any others will pray for me, my wife, my mother and my father. Oh, the power of it, and the humbling of it! It makes a man feel that he must be in line with such praying, and he is afraid. ⟨ Yet it makes him strong for he knows that " more things are wrought by prayer than this world dreams of."⟩ Oh, for the multiplication of those who will devote themselves to this special labour of intercession.

With all that we have attempted to consider in our minds, we lift our faces to the face of our Lord as did the men who watched Him pray in the olden days, and say to Him, "Lord, teach us to pray."

Lightning Source UK Ltd.
Milton Keynes UK
UKHW051819140223
416720UK00010B/587